Practical Guide to the Operational Use of the DShK Machine Gun – 3rd Edition

By Erik Lawrence

Copyright ©2014 Erik Lawrence

Erik Lawrence

www.vig-sec.com   erik@vig-sec.com

Printed and bound in the United States of America

First printing 2006
Second printing 2009
Third printing 2014

ISBN-10: 1-941998-03-8
ISBN-13: 978-1-941998-03-8
E-BOOK-ISBN-13: 978-1-941998-22-9
LCCN: Not yet assigned

I0170704

ATTENTION US MILITARY UNITS, US GOVERNMENT AGENCIES AND PROFESSIONAL ORGANIZATIONS: Quantity discounts are available on bulk purchases of this book. Special books or book excerpts can also be created to fit specific needs. For information, please contact:

Erik Lawrence

www.vig-sec.com   erik@vig-sec.com

Training should be received from knowledgeable and experienced operators on this particular weapons system. Vigilant Security Services provides this training and continually perfects its instruction with up-to-date information from actual use.

CREDITS:
Wikipedia contributors, "Main Page," Wikipedia, The Free Encyclopedia,
http://en.wikipedia.org/w/index.php?title=Main_Page&oldid=83971314
(accessed October 7, 2006).

Firearms are potentially dangerous and must be handled responsibly by individuals. The technical information presented in this manual on the use of the DShK Machine Gun reflects the author's research, beliefs, and experiences. The information in this book is presented for academic study only. Neither the author nor the publisher assumes any responsibility for the use or misuse of information contained in this book.

SAFETY NOTICE
Before starting an inspection, ensure the weapon is cleared. Do not manipulate the trigger until the weapon has been cleared of all ammunition. Inspect the chamber to ensure that it is empty and no ammunition is present. Keep the weapon oriented in a safe direction when loading and handling.

AMMUNITION NOTICE- this weapon fires the 12.7 x 108 mm Soviet, not the 12.7 x 99 mm (US .50 BMG). Firing the incorrect ammunition will damage the weapon and possibly injure the operator/assistant operator.

www.vig-sec.com

PREFACE

This manual is intended to be a reference for those involved in the use, maintenance and instruction of the featured firearm. My aim in writing these manuals is to set the record straight and dispel many of the false assumptions related to the different firearms. The early sections of the manual contain background material on the featured firearm which allows the user to gain the basic building blocks for further education. The firearms featured in these manuals have been used for decades by our allies and enemies, and will be for the foreseeable future, so why are we not experts with them? If I am fighting with the firearm or providing instruction on a firearm, I want to use and know their system better than they do.

The rationale for writing these manuals comes from the fact that there are not libraries of easily accessible references to use in developing your own training system for these firearms. Many of the old military field manuals are decades old and were incorrectly translated by someone who had no idea what the firearm could do, let alone basic firearm knowledge. We started from the ground up and developed the manuals to provide instruction in progressive steps that could be easily grasped and continually referred back to. A good grounding in the basics of firearms, safety, and instruction allows the user to use these manuals to their maximum value. A competent user will find little difficulty in interpreting and applying the information in the manual to their own training program.

The guide goes through the most fundamental parts of the firearm in detail and more advanced techniques are not covered as extensively. With this in mind the user can use these principles and adapt it as needed to their required level of instruction. The emphasis of this guide is in acquiring familiarity with the fundamentals of all firearms and learned competence rather than becoming a firearms guru.

Many of the points in these guides were developed from scratch in theatres of conflict and are continually improved and updated for each edition. I have continually used vetted points from users and professionals in the guides to continually update them to the best known practices for each particular firearm. If it is valid and relevant we will include it in the next edition.

Please note that this guide assumes some familiarity with the basic concepts in firearm safety, gun handling skills, common sense and an ability to process new information. Readers should have knowledge of the difference in calibers, countries of origin, and the knowledge of the priority of the skills needed for development.

I hope you find this work useful and remember that a manual does not replace proper training and hands on experience. Please email comments to <u>erik@vig-sec.com</u> , particularly if you find any errors or glaring omissions.

Erik Lawrence

Table of Contents

Section 1 1

  Introduction 1

    Description.. 1

    Background... 2

    Variants 3

Section 2.. 10

  Maintenance 10

  Clearing the DShKM 13

    Disassembling the DShKM MG 17

    Reassembling the DShKM MG 23

    Performing a Function Check on the DShKM MG 27

    Disassembling the Barrel and Gas Regulator.. 28

    Reassembling the DShKM MG Barrel 32

Section 3.. 37

  Operation and Function.. 37

    Setting up and mounting the DShKM on the tripod................................... 37

    Loading the DShKM MG 45

    Firing the DShKM MG 47

    Unloading the DShKM MG.. 49

Section 4.. 55

  Performance Problems... 55

    Malfunction and Immediate Action Procedures.. 55

Appendix A - Ammunition.. 58

Appendix B - Ammunition Comparison.. 62

Appendix C – Munitions Packaging Markings.. 63

Appendix D – Manufacturer ID Markings 66

Appendix E- Non-Standard Weapons Theory... 68

Appendix F- Tools and Training Tips.. 71

Appendix G- Good to know additional information 72

DShK
12.7mm
Heavy Machine Gun

3rd Edition

Section 1

Introduction

The objective of this manual is to allow the reader to be able to competently use the DShK weapon systems. The manual will give the reader background/specifications of the weapon, instruct on its operation, disassembly and assembly, proper firing procedure, and malfunction/misfire procedures. Operator level maintenance will also be detailed to allow the reader to fully understand and become competent in the use and maintenance of the DShK Machine Gun.

Description

The **ДШК**, for *Дегтярёва Шпагина Крупнокалиберный, Degtyaryova Shpagina Krupnokalibernyy, Degtyarev-Shpagin "Large-Caliber" 12.7mm Krupnocalibernyj Pulemeot Degtyareva-Shpagina*, (**DShK**) is an automatic heavy machine gun, designed in the late 1930s by Russian firearms designer Degtyarev. This operator's manual will educate the reader as to basic operations and descriptions on this weapon system.

DShK was one of the most successful designs of its time. 12.7mm AP bullets fired from that MG, could pierce a 15mm armor plate at 500m.

DShK is the belt-fed, air-cooled, gas-operated weapon that fires only in full-automatic mode. The gas system has a 3 positions gas regulator for tuning the amount of gas introduced into the operating system. The bolt is locked in the receiver via two horizontally pivoted locking flaps attached to the bolt. The overall system is similar to the RP46 and the DP-27 light machine gun, but (scaled up) and with the addition of the bolt and bolt carrier buffer assemblies in the receiver back plate. The original belt-feed system, designed by Shpagin, used a non-disintegrating belt with open pockets. To delink the cartridges prior to chamber them, Shpagin used a rotary drum that fed the belt and pulled the cartridges out of their belt pockets simultaneously. The drum was operated via the oscillating arm, that, in turn, was operated by the charging handle, rigidly attached to the bolt carrier. Belts were inserted at the top of the feed module, and cartridges were caught by the bolt and chambered at the bottom of the feed. Belts were fed from the left side of the gun and the belts came in 50-round belt units. The DShK featured a non-quick-detach heavy barrel with radial fins to improve cooling and a large and effective muzzle brake.

The DShK was used on a wheeled universal mount, which was fitted with a removable steel shield. This mount allowed for anti-aircraft (AA) usage; for AA roles the wheels were removed and a mount "tail" was separated and formed a folding tripod. A special shoulder stock and AA sight were also attached for Air Defense role. Some DShKs were used on pintle mounts on small ships.

The DShKM was more or less the same weapon, with the most distinctive change being the different belt feed, distinguished by its much flatter and square-outlined appearance. This feed module also used an oscillating arm linked to the charging handle to operate feed.

The DShK and DShKM were quite adequate weapons for the time period they appeared in, but these guns were too heavy, and too complicated to manufacture, and reliability in severe conditions was slightly less than desired, so they were replaced by much better designs in the Soviet/Russian military.

Background

The first Soviet heavy-caliber machine gun was designed on official request as a dedicated anti-aircraft weapon. A request was issued to designer Vasily Degtyarev (who already designed a DP-27 LMG) in 1929. The first prototype of the 12.7mm machine gun, named DK (*Degtyarev, Krupnocalibernyj - Degtyarev*, Large caliber) was built in 1930. This gun was officially adopted, and the DK was manufactured in small numbers from 1933-1935. It was a gas-operated weapon, firing the powerful 12.7mm cartridge, but with magazine feeding. The drum magazine held only 30 rounds and was bulky and heavy, and the practical rate of fire was unsatisfactory low. In the late 1930s, another famous Soviet arms designer, Shpagin, designed an add-on belt feed system that could be easily installed on the DK.

The modification appeared in 1938, and in 1939 it was officially adopted by the Red Army as a *12.7mm Krupnocalibernyj Pulemet Degtyareva-Shpagina*, DShK (*Degtyarev-Shpagin, large caliber*). The DShK was used through WWII as an anti-aircraft weapon and also as a heavy infantry support gun. It also had been used on some heavy Soviet tanks as a roof-mounted AA gun. After the war some care had been taken to improve the DShK; and a rotary belt-fed unit was replaced by a more conventional slide-operated one, some other improvements also were made. The DShK 1938 was used in several roles. As an anti-aircraft weapon, it was mounted on pintle and tripod mounts and on a triple mount on the GAZ-AA truck. Late in the war, it was mounted on the cupolas of IS-2 tanks and ISU-152 self-propelled guns. As an infantry heavy-support weapon, it used a two-wheeled trolley, similar to that developed by Sokolov for the 1910 Maxim gun. It was also mounted in vehicle turrets, for example, in the T-40 light amphibious tank.

The new weapon was adopted as a DShKM, or DShK Modernized, and is also known as DShKM-38/46. It also was used as an infantry heavy-support/AA-gun and mounted on some tanks and armored vehicles (T-55, T-62, and BTR-155). In the late 1960s and 1970s, the DShKM was gradually replaced in Soviet Army service by the more modern NSV/NSVT machine gun. The DShKM was widely exported to Soviet-friendly nations and regimes. It was also manufactured in other countries, such as China, Iran, Yugoslavia, Romania and Pakistan. It was widely used in numerous insurgencies, including Afghan campaigns.

Variants

DShK-38

Figure 1-1 DShK-38

A. Country of Origin: USSR/Russia

B. Military Designation:
   DShK 38 (*Krupnocalibernyj Pulemet Degtyareva-Shpagina*)

C. Cartridge Type: <u>12.7mm X 108mm</u> cartridge

D. Type of Feed: Belt-fed rotary type

E. Locking System: None

F. System of Operation: Gas operated

G. Range:
   a. Maximum effective range: 3,830 yards (3,500m)
   b. Maximum range: 5,900 yards (5,400m)
   c. Maximum AA ceiling: 8,200 feet (2,500m)

H. Weight: 34 kg/75 pounds machine gun and barrel
   a. 167 kg/368 pounds on universal wheeled mount

I. Length: 1625 mm/64 inches

J. Length of barrel: 1000 mm / 39 inches

K. Metallic non-disintegrating, Belts: 50 rounds in metal can

L. Rate of fire: 575 rounds/min

M. Velocity: 850 meters per second/2790 feet per second

DShKM-38/46

Figure 1-2 DShKM-38/46

A. Country of Origin: USSR/Russia

B. Military Designation: **DShKM 38/46** (*Krupnocalibernyj Pulemet Degtyareva-Shpagina Modernized*)

C. Cartridge Type: <u>12.7mm X 108mm</u> cartridge

D. Type of Feed: Belt-fed lever type

E. Locking System: None

F. System of Operation: Gas operated

N. Range:
   a. Maximum effective range: 3,830 yards (3,500m)
   b. Maximum range: 5,900 yards (5,400m)
   c. Maximum AA ceiling: 8,200 feet (2,500m)

O. Weight: 36.3 kg/80 pounds, machine gun and barrel
   a. 157 kg/346 pounds on universal wheeled mount

P. Length: 1625 mm/64 inches

Q. Length of barrel: 1070 mm/42 inches

R. Belts: Metallic non-disintegrating, 50 rounds in metal can

S. Rate of fire: 600 rounds/min

T. Velocity: 855 meters per second/2805 feet per second

Other Official Designations

Single Mount   DShK or DShKM

Twin Open Mount   DShKM-2

Quad Mount   DShKM-4

Single Open Turret   MTU-2

Twin Open Turret   MSTU

Twin Armored Turret   DShKM-2B

Figure 1-3 DShK in tripod configuration

DShK in Anti Aircraft Mode

The infantry version of the machine gun, which is mounted to the two-wheel chassis, can be opened out to form a tall tripod for engaging aircraft.

Figure 1-4 DShKM DShK machine gun mounted on a Russian tank

Figure 1-5 DShKM in tripod mode

Type 77 Heavy Machine Gun

Figure 1-6 Chinese Type 77

The Type 77 was type classified in 1977, and its production began in 1980. A large number of the Type 77 Anti Aircraft Machine Gun (AAMGs) were equipped to the Chinese PLA to replace the obsolete Type 54. The Type 77 is an automatic, belt-fed, recoil-operated, air-cooled, crew-operated machine gun. The gun can be fitted with a 2X optical aiming sight. The machine gun is mounted on an adjustable-height tripod and can be carried by soldiers with limited ammunitions over short distances.

A. Country of Origin: China

B. Military Designation: **Type 77**

C. Cartridge Type: 12.7mm X 108mm cartridge

D. Type of Feed: Belt-fed lever type

E. System of Operation: Recoil operated

F. Range
    a. Maximum effective range: 2,830 yards (2,500m)
    b. Maximum range: 4,900 yards (4,400m)
    c. Maximum AA ceiling: 8,200 feet (2,500m)

G. Weight:
    a. 56 kg/125.5 pounds, machine gun and barrel
    b. 28.3 kg/62.4 pounds for tripod

      c. 21.3 kg/47 pounds for barrel

H. Length: 2150 mm/84.6 inches

I. Length of barrel: 1605 mm/63 inches

J. Belts: Metallic non-disintegrating

K. Rate of fire:
      a. 650-700 rounds per minute (maximum)
      b. 60-100 rounds per minute (sustained)

L. Velocity: 825 meters per second/2706 feet per second

Type 54 (Type 59) Antiaircraft Machine Gun

Figure 1-7 Chinese Type 54

The **Type 54** is a Chinese copy of the Soviet DShK M38/46 Machine Gun. The weapon was type classified in 1954 and was equipped to the Chinese PLA in a huge number. Most Type 54s have been retired from service since the 1970s and were replaced by the Type 77 AAMG.

China has also developed a vehicle-mounted variant of the Type 54, which has been fitted on almost all tanks and armored vehicles in service with the PLA before the late 1980s. This variant was designated as **Type 59** and has the same design as the Type 54 (and therefore sometimes is also referred as Type 54 by foreign reports).

The Type 54/59 is basically a World War II-era automatic, belt-fed, recoil operated, air-cooled, crew-operated machine gun. The Type 54 received some modifications after entering service, including the improved tripod and a reduced combat weight from 127.5 kg to 53 kg.

    A. Country of Origin: China

    B. Military Designation: **Type 54**

    C. Cartridge Type: <u>12.7mm X 108mm</u> cartridge

    D. Type of Feed: Belt fed lever type

    E. System of Operation: Recoil operated

Section 2

Maintenance

Figure 2-1 DShKM Disassemble, complete

Figure 2-2 DShKM Safety

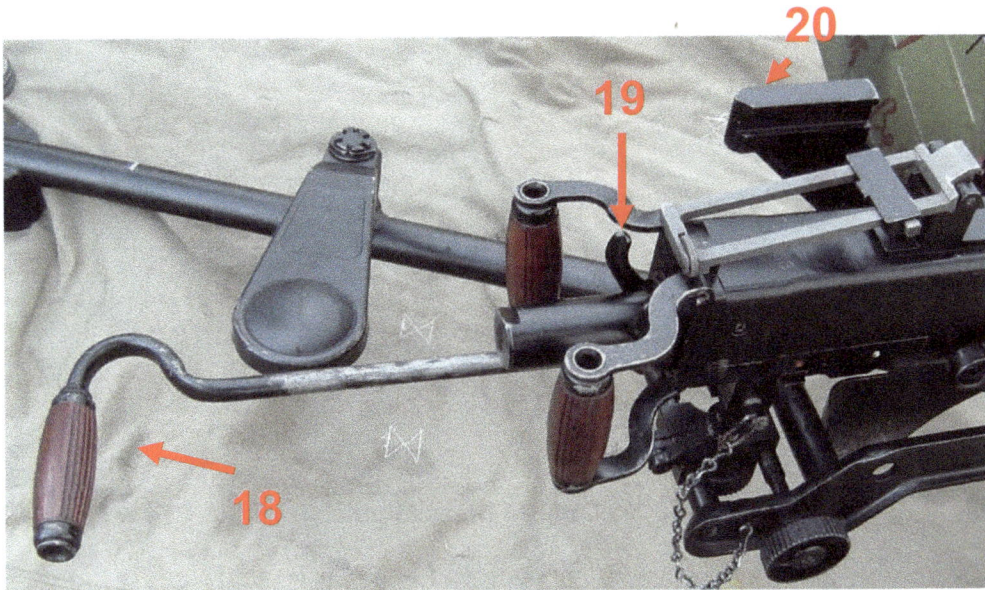

Figure 2-3 DShKM Rear of receiver

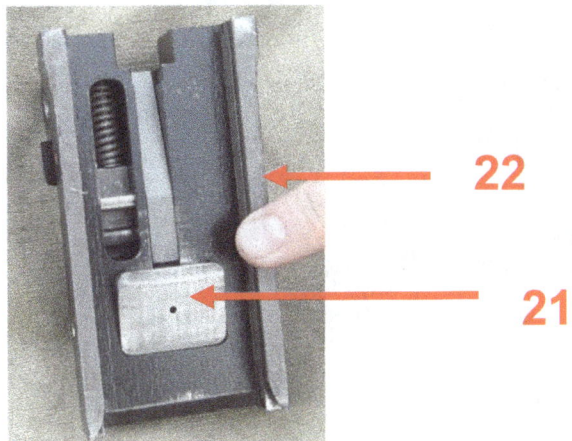

Figure 2-4 DShKM Sear Assembly

Figure 2-5 DShKM Disassemble, Slide Assembly

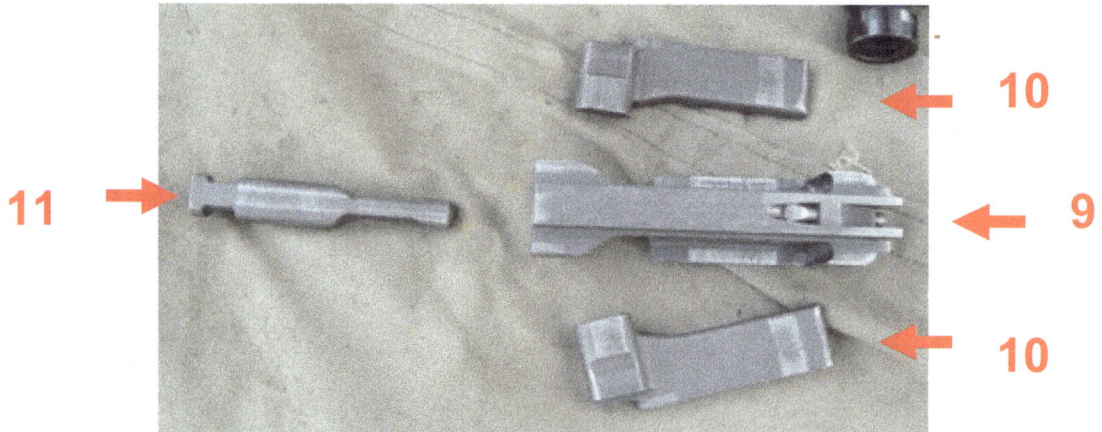

Figure 2-6 DShKM Disassemble, Bolt

Figure 2-7a Barrel Removal

Figure 2-7b Barrel nut and lock

1- Rear Sight	2- Feed Tray	3- Feed Operating Lever
4- Feed Tray Cover	5- Barrel Carrying Handle	6- Front Sight
7- Muzzle Brake	8- Slide and Piston Rod Assembly	
9- Bolt	10- Bolt Locking Flaps	11- Firing Pin Actuator
12- Sear Assembly	13- Retaining Pin	14- Backplate
15- Receiver	16- Safety Lever	17- Tripod Mounting Pin Grip
18- Operating Rod	19- Trigger	20- AA Sight Mount
21- Sear	22- Sear Assembly	23- Barrel Lock
24- Barrel Nut	25- Barrel Nut Lock	

Clearing the DShKM

Figure 2-8 Operating rod

A. Pull the bolt to the rear by the charging handle (Figure 2-8).

Figure 2-9 Safety lever

B. Ensure the weapon is on safe, safety lever forward (Figure 2-9).

Figure 2-9 Feed tray catch

C. Open the feed tray cover by pushing the cover catch (Figure 2-9).

Figure 2-10 Remove ammunition and belt

D. Lift up the feed tray cover; remove any belt in the mechanism (Figure 2-10).

Figure 2-11 Opening the feed tray

E. Lift up the feed tray; remove any round in the mechanism (Figure 2-11).

Figure 2-12 Inspecting the chamber

F. Inspect the face of the bolt and chamber to ensure it is clear of ammunition (Figure 2-12).

G. Rotate the safety to fire

H. Holding the operating handle, press the trigger and ease the bolt forward, then place back on safe.

NOTE: you may use the method below if the charging handle is not operating.

Figure 2-13 Expedient operating rod

1. Use a spent casing to actuate the bolt by inserting the rear of the casing into the exposed bolt receptacle (Figure 2-13).

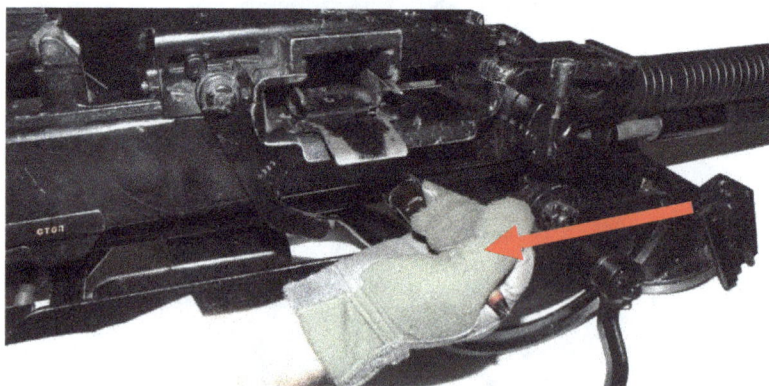

Figure 2-14 Expedient operating rod usage

2. Pull the bolt to the rear or ride it forward on the empty chamber (Figure 2-14).

I. Close the cover and lower the rear sight.

Disassembling the DShKM MG

NOTE: Place the weapon's parts on a flat, clean surface with the muzzle oriented in a safe direction.

When the operator begins to disassemble the weapon, it should be done in the following order:

A. Ensure the weapon is clear, the rear sight raised, the weapon is off the SAFE position, and the feed-tray cover and feed tray are open.

Figure 2-15 Backplate retaining pin

B. Locate the backplate retaining (Figure 2-15).

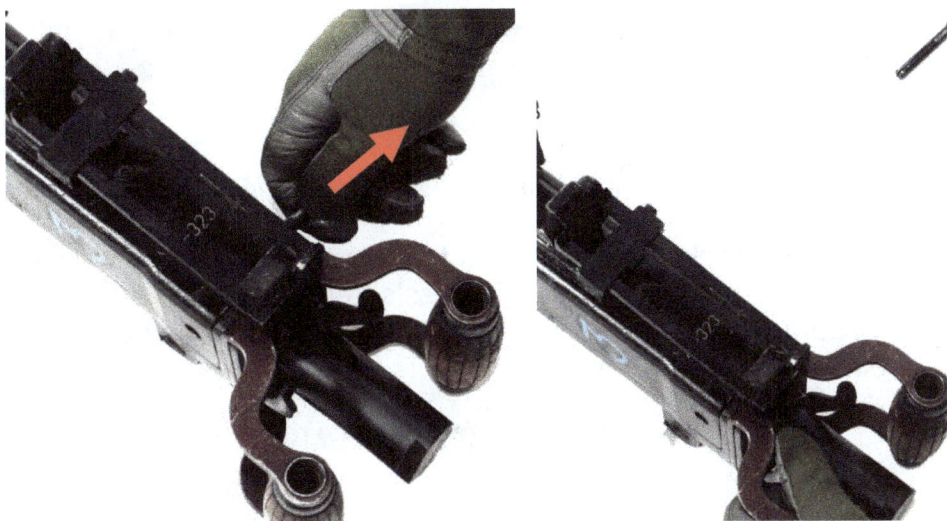

Figure 2-16 Removal of backplate retaining pin

C. Drive out the backplate retaining pin, from right to left or left to right depending on its orientation, with a drift pin until it separates from the receiver and set the pin aside (Figure 2-16).

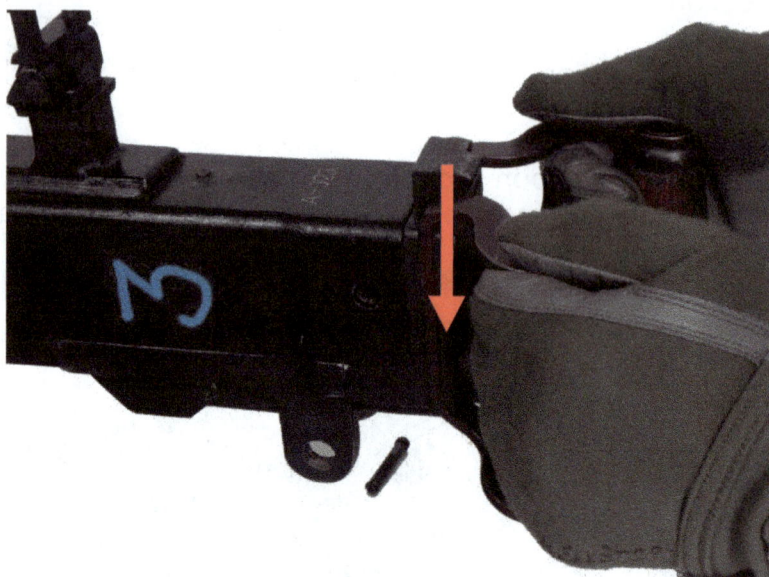

Figure 2-17a Backplate removal

Figure 2-17b Backplate removal

Figure 2-17c Pin retention

D. Drive the backplate downward to remove it from the receiver. You may need to use a rubber mallet to assist, ensure to fold the rear sight forward (upright). This is a good time to replace the backplate retaining pin into the backplate to prevent its loss. (Figures 2-17a - 2-17c).

Figure 2-17a Backplate removal

Figure 2-18 Sear assembly removal

D. Remove the sear assembly by sliding it to the rear of the receiver (Figure 2-18).

Figure 2-19 Sear assembly inspection

E. Inspect the sear for damage – chipped or cracked sear. Check the spring tension of the safety disconnect while checking the SAFE/FIRE function. (Figure 2-19).

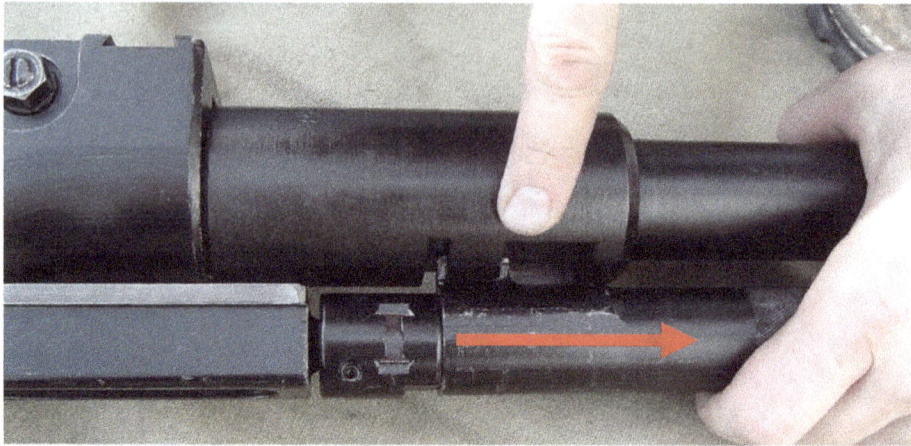

Figure 2-20a Gas piston removal

Figure 2-20b Gas piston removal

E. Hold the serrated portion of the gas piston cover, which is under the barrel, and slide it forward. Once it is fully forward, turn the piston cover to separate it from the barrel (Figures 2-20a and 2-20b).

Figure 2-21 Slide and piston assembly

F. Pull the operating slide assembly stud rearward and remove the gas piston, bolt, operating slide, and gas-piston tube from the receiver.

Figure 2-22 bolt assembly removal

G. Lift the bolt off the operating slide (Figure 2-22).

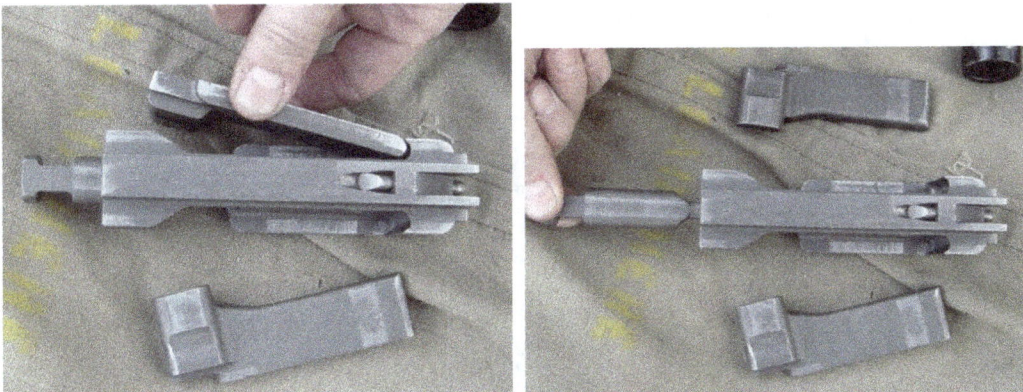

Figure 2-23 Locking flaps and firing pin removal

H. Remove the locking flaps and firing pin (Figure 2-23).

Figure 2-24 Extractor inspection

I. On the bolt face, inspect the extractor for chips, burrs, or lack of spring tension (Figure 2-24).

Figure 2-25 Ejector inspection

J. On the bolt face, inspect the ejector for chips, burrs, or lack of spring tension (Figure 2-25).

Figure 2-26 Operator-level disassembled weapon

Reassembling the DShKM MG

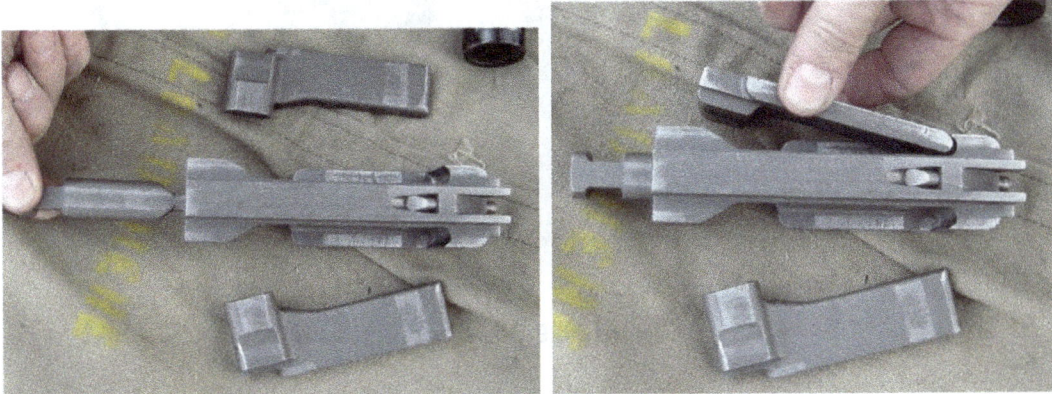

Figure 2-27 Bolt assembly

A. Insert the firing pin and realign the locking flaps onto the bolt. Maintain an orientation so that the extractor is to the bottom (Figure 2-27).

Figure 2-28 Bolt assembly onto slide

B. Align the bolt onto the operating slide. Push the bolt assembly forward on the slide until the locking flaps lie flush against the bolt (Figure 2-28).

Figure 2-29 Slide and piston assembly

Figure 2-30 Fully inserted slide and piston assembly in receiver

C. Insert the slide and gas-piston assembly forward into the receiver. The second photo is of the underside of the bolt which is fully forward in the receiver (Figure 2-30).

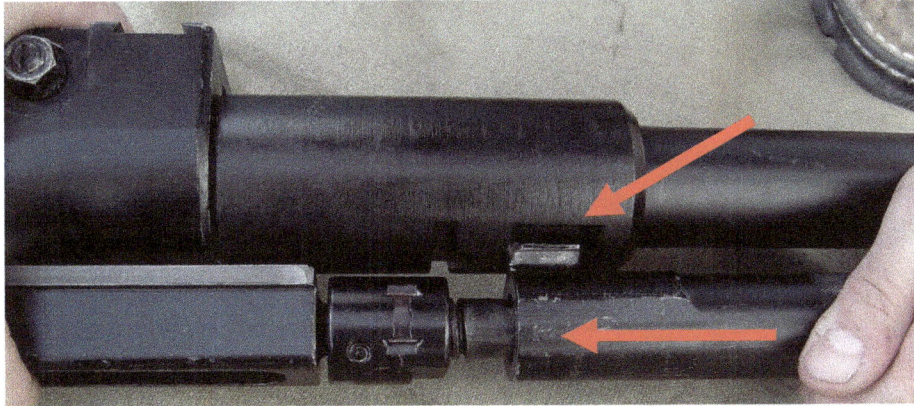

Figure 2-31a Piston installation

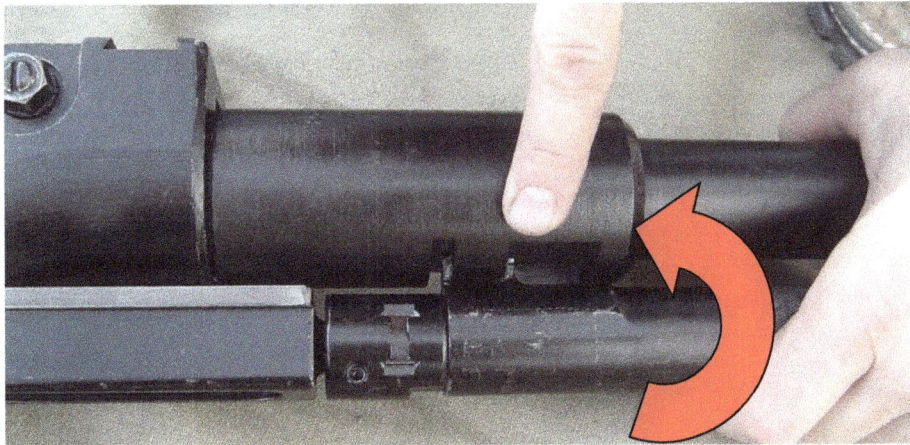

Figure 2-31b Piston installation

D. Hold the serrated portion of the gas piston cover which is under the barrel and slide it forward. Once it is fully forward turn the piston cover to insert it into the barrel. Now release the tension on the gas piston cover (Figures 2-31a and 2-31b).

Figure 2-32a Sear assembly installation

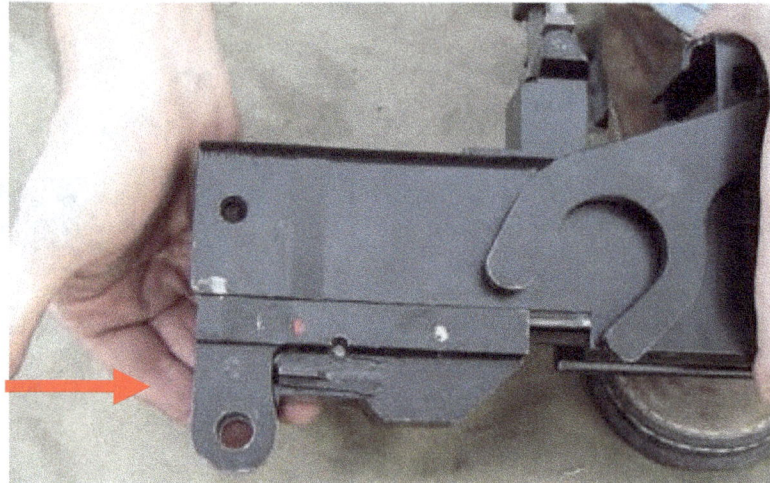

Figure 2-32b Sear assembly installation

E. Insert the sear assembly by sliding it to the rear of the receiver till it stops (Figures 2-32a and 2-32b).

Figure 2-33 Backplate installation

F. From the bottom of the receiver, start the backplate in the grooves and tap it up until it lines up with the hole for the retaining pin (Figure 2-33).

Figure 2-34 Backplate retaining pin installation

J. Insert the backplate retaining pin from left to right; align the receiver hole with the backplate hole with a drift pin if necessary.

NOTE: Check the receiver to ensure the feed operating lever is pushed forward before closing the cover.

K. Close the feed tray cover and lower the rear sight.

Performing a Function Check on the DShKM MG

A. Ensure the weapon is clear of any ammunition.

B. Pull the operating handle till the bolt locks to the rear.

C. Ensure the safety is forward to the safe position.

D. Pull the trigger; bolt should not go forward.

E. Rotate the safety rearward (fire).

F. Pull the charging handle to the rear, or with an expended casing, hold the operating rod to the rear and pull trigger. The bolt should be released forward; do this step gently and do not let it slam onto an empty chamber.

Disassembling the Barrel and Gas Regulator

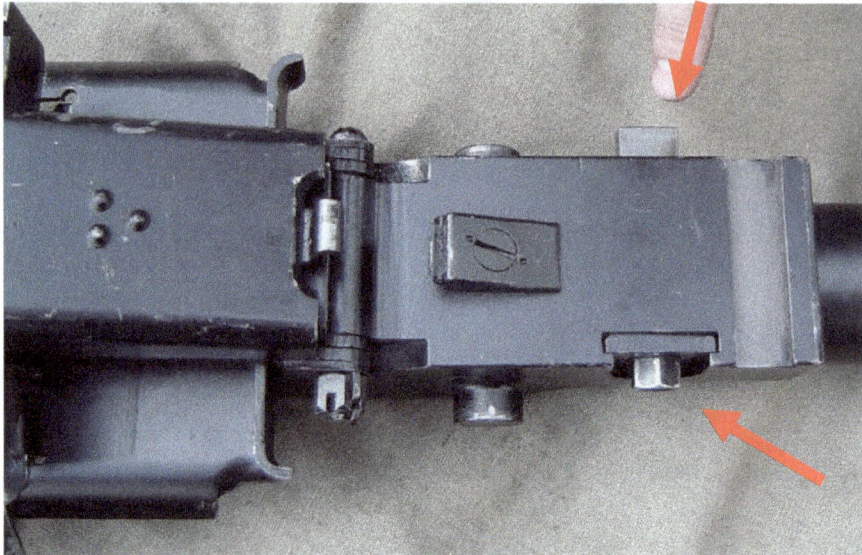

Figure 2-35 Barrel nut and barrel lock

A. Locate the barrel lock and barrel nut (Figure 2-35).

Figure 2-36 Barrel nut removal

B. Loosen the barrel nut on the right side of the receiver (Figure 2-36).

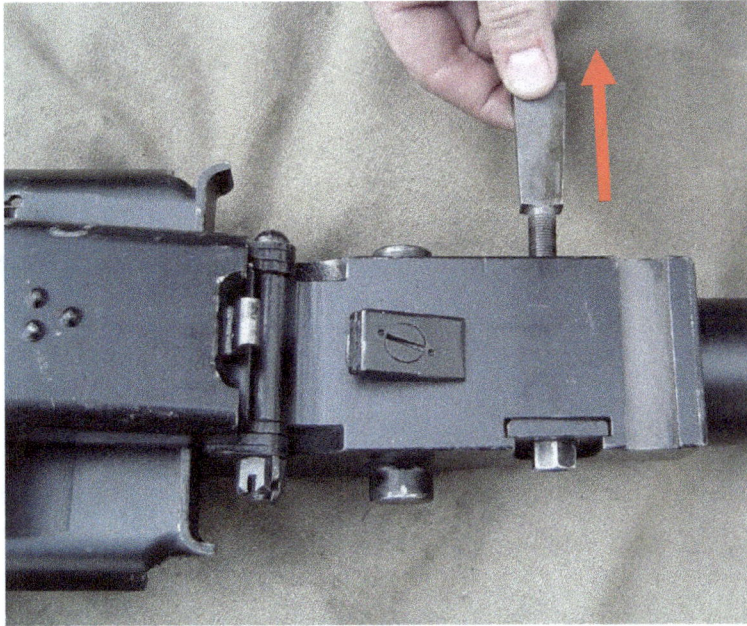

Figure 2-37 Barrel lock removal

C. Remove the barrel lock; notice the tapered wedge-like sides. These wedges are how different barrels uniformly lock up when tightened (Figure 2-37).

Figure 2-38 Barrel nut and lock removal

D. Slide up the barrel nut lock and barrel nut. If you are just changing barrels during use you do not need to do this step, just pull the barrel and replace it. Once the new barrel is in the receiver replace the barrel lock and tighten the nut (Figure 2-38).

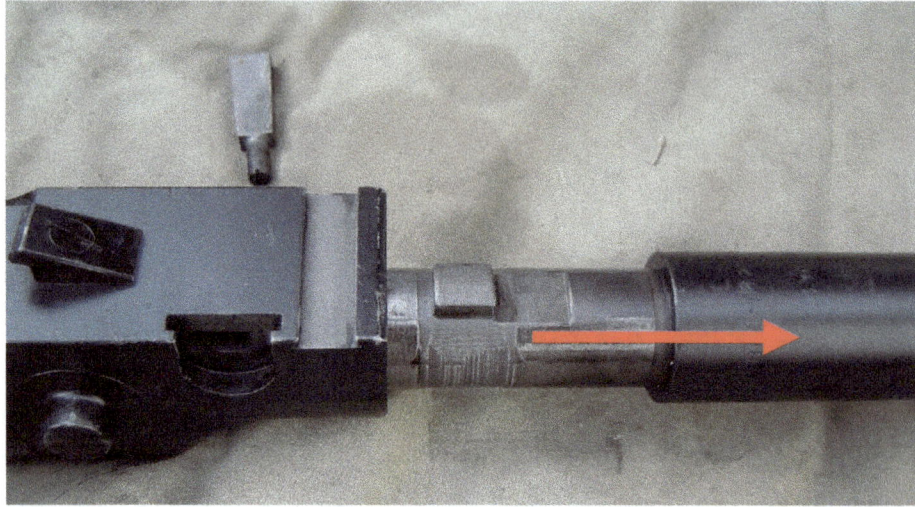

Figure 2-39 Barrel removal

E. Pull the barrel from the receiver (Figure 2-39).

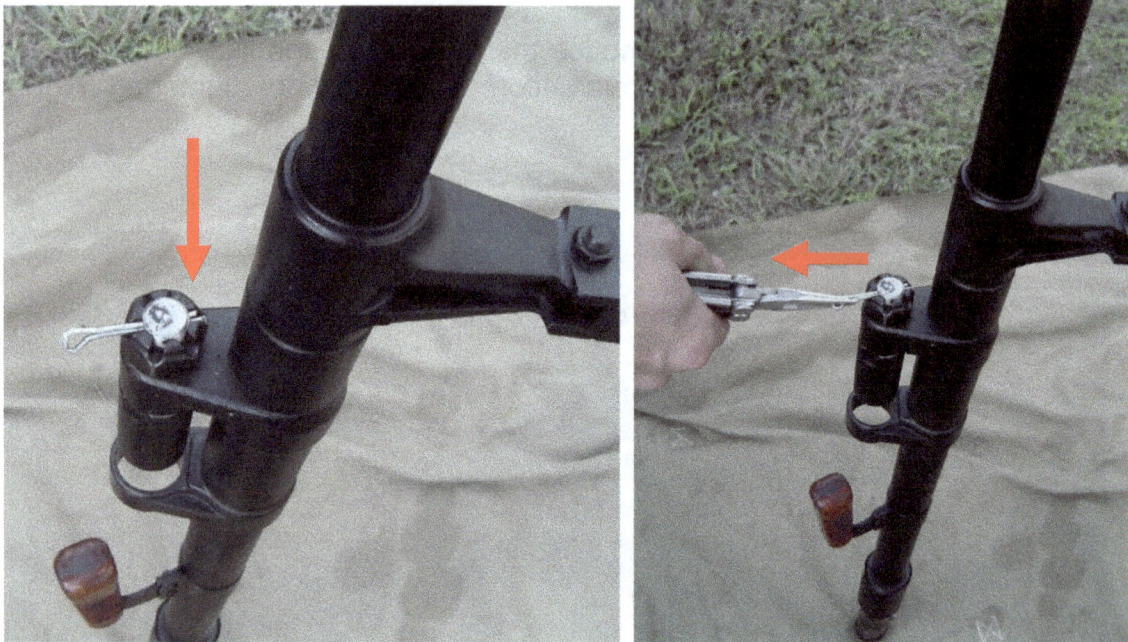

Figure 2-40a & 2-40b Gas regulator cotter pin removal

F. Straighten the ends of the cotter pin on the gas regulator and remove the cotter pin.

Figure 2-41a & 2-41b Gas regulator nut removal

G. Loosen the gas regulator bolt and remove it.

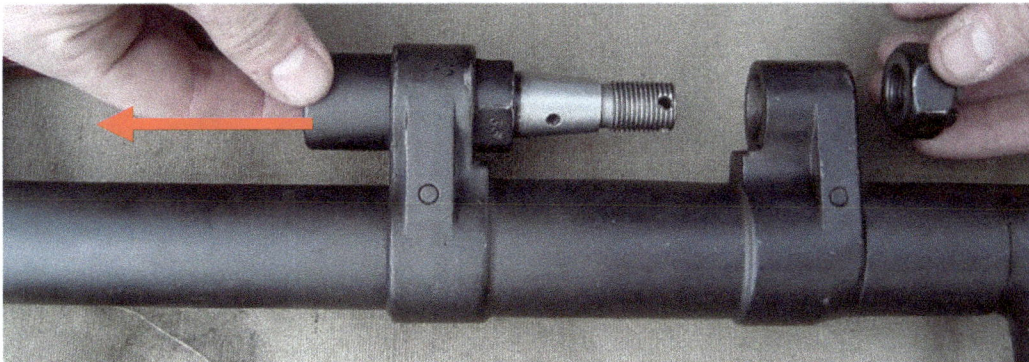

Figure 2-42 Gas regulator removal

Figure 2-43 Gas regulator

H. Remove the gas regulator by sliding it back through the piston guide.

Reassembling the DShKM MG Barrel

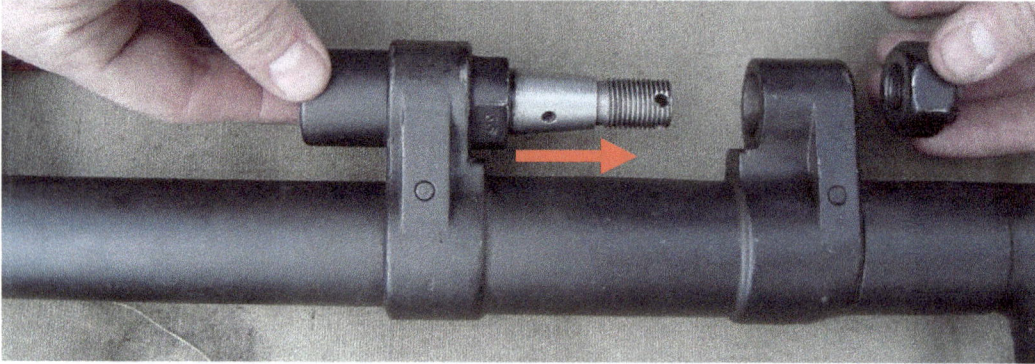

Figure 2-44 Gas regulator installation

A. Reinsert the gas regulator by sliding it back through the piston guide. There are three gas settings for this weapon, numbered 3, 3.5, 4 (the higher the number, the more gas introduced into the system). This regulator should be set to the lowest gas setting that will allow it still to function reliably.

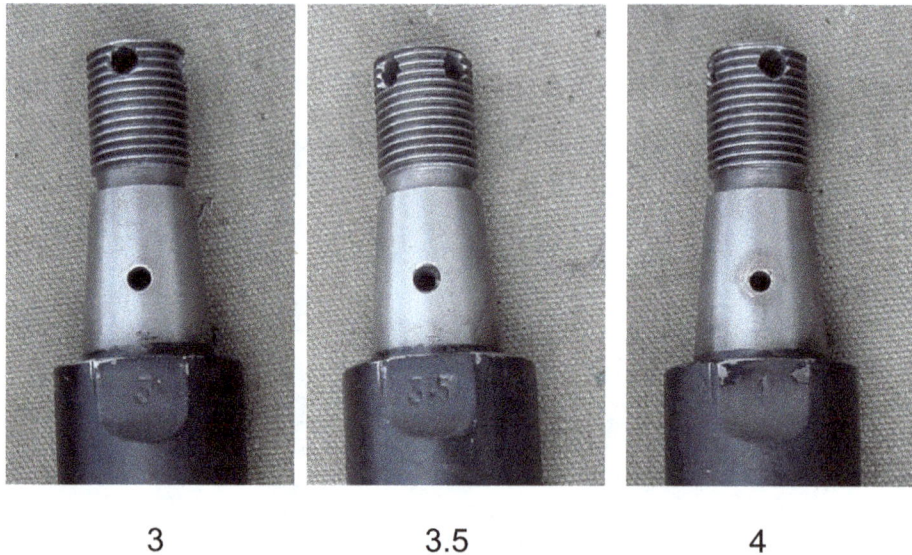

| 3 | 3.5 | 4 |

Figure 2-45 Gas regulator settings

Figure 2-46 Gas vent hole

1. Align the appropriate number on the gas regulator with the gas vent hole on the barrel when reinstalling the gas regulator (Figures 2-45 and 2-46).

Figure 2-47 Gas regulator nut installation

B. Start and tighten the gas-regulator bolt; do not over tighten. Line up a hole for the cotter pin (Figure 2-47).

Figure 2-48a & 2-48b Gas regulator cotter pin installation

C. Push the cotter pin fully through the lined-up nut-locking hole and bend the pins out around the nut (Figure 2-48a and 2-48b).

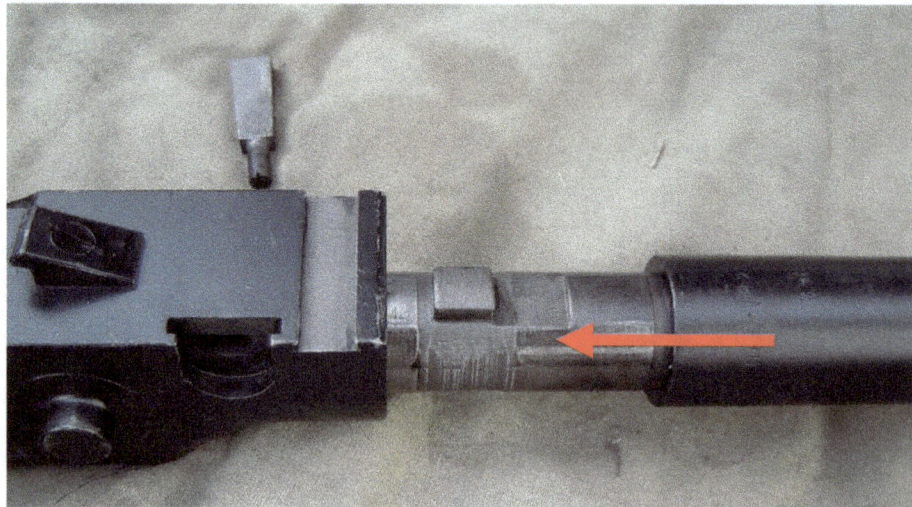

Figure 2-49 Barrel installation

D. Push the barrel into the front of the receiver, locking notch up (Figure 2-49).

Figure 2-50 Barrel nut and lock installation

E. Slide down the barrel nut lock with barrel nut (Figure 2-50).

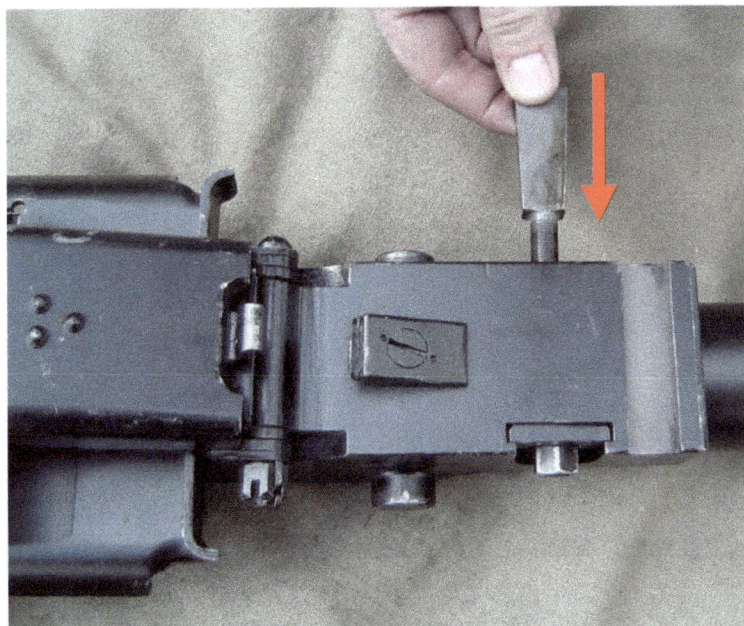

Figure 2-51 Barrel lock insertion

F. Reinsert the barrel-lock; notice the tapered wedge-like sides and flat top and bottom. These wedges are how different barrels uniformly lock up when tightened. Push it fully in, with gently taps if needed, until it reaches the threads of the bolt (Figure 2-51).

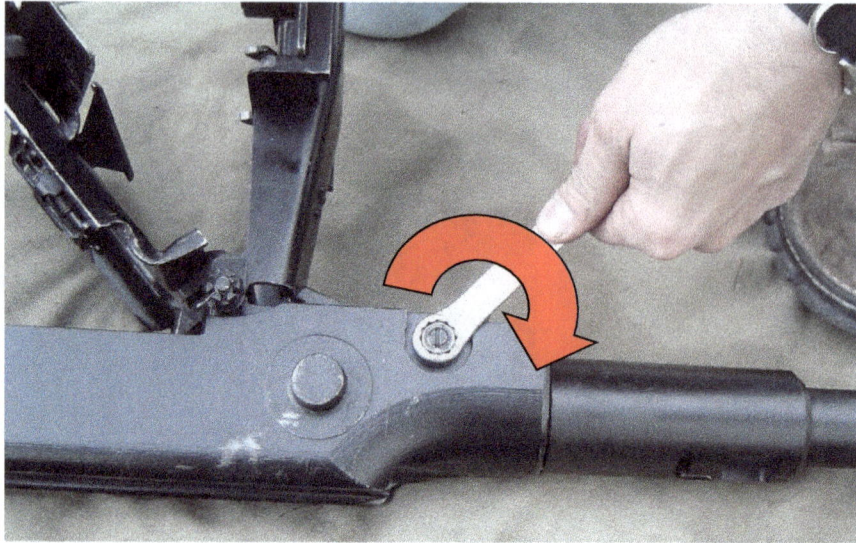

Figure 2-52 Barrel nut tightening

G. Tighten the barrel nut on the right side of the receiver; do not over tighten (Figure 2-52).

H. Barrel assembly is complete.

Section 3

Operation and Function

Setting up and mounting the DShKM on the tripod

Figure 3-1 Tripod Components

1- Gun Cradle   2- Locking Ring   3- Tripod

Figure 3-2 Front log extension

A. Lift the center leg, depress the spring-loaded latch and pull the bottom of the tripod leg to full extension and lock the latch (Figure 3-2).

Figure 3-3 Tripod positioning and securing

B. Loosen each joint and rotate the remaining two legs out to form the height of tripod you desire. Once it is the height you desire, lock the joints, but be careful to level the mounting platform. Sandbag or spike down the legs if you have them to assist in making the firing position stable. Face the center leg that you first extended towards the intended firing direction (Figure 3-3).

Figure 3-4 Lock ring

C. Place the gun cradle onto the tripod platform and align it so the lock ring will go around and tighten to mate the tripod to the gun cradle (Figure 3-4).

Figure 3-5a Tightened lock ring

D. Rotate the locking tab to the receiving side of the locking ring and tighten. Do not over tighten the lock ring at this time; it will need to be tightened prior to firing (Figure 3-5a and 3-5b).

Figure 3-5b Tripod with cradle installed

E. Next the weapon can be mounted to the gun cradle. Open the locking tabs on the top of the cradle to receive the studs on the side of the weapon receiver.

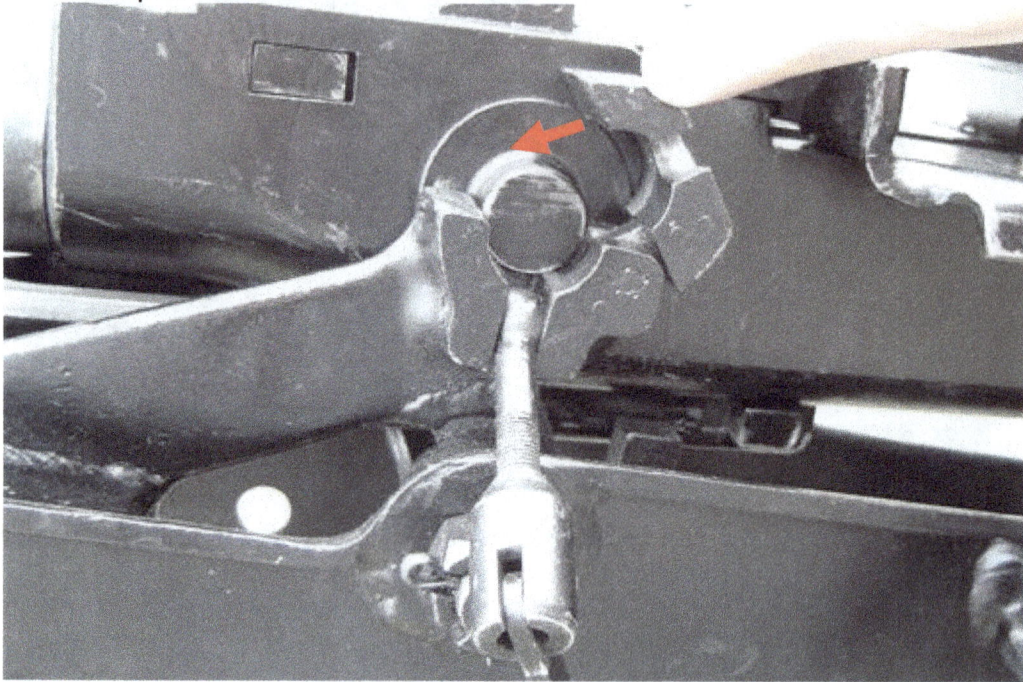

Figure 3-6 Gun to cradle mating

F. Set the studs on the sides of the receiver into the receptacles and close both hinged covers (Figure 3-6).

Figure 3-7 Operating rod stud and slide assembly stud alignment

G. Rotate and tighten the locks on either side. Note that the charging handle stud (lower), which is located on the end of the charging handle that is mounted to the cradle, must be in front of the stud on the bottom of the bolt (upper). This arrangement allows the charging handle on the cradle to be used to manipulate the bolt (Figure 3-7).

Figure 3-8 Mounting rear of receiver to cradle

H. Align the rear mounting bracket with the mounting brackets on the cradle (Figure 3-8).

Figure 3-9 Rear mounting pin

I. Insert the lock pin into the brackets from left to right… (Figure 3-9).

Figure 3-10 Fully seated pin

J. and fully seat it (Figure 3-10).

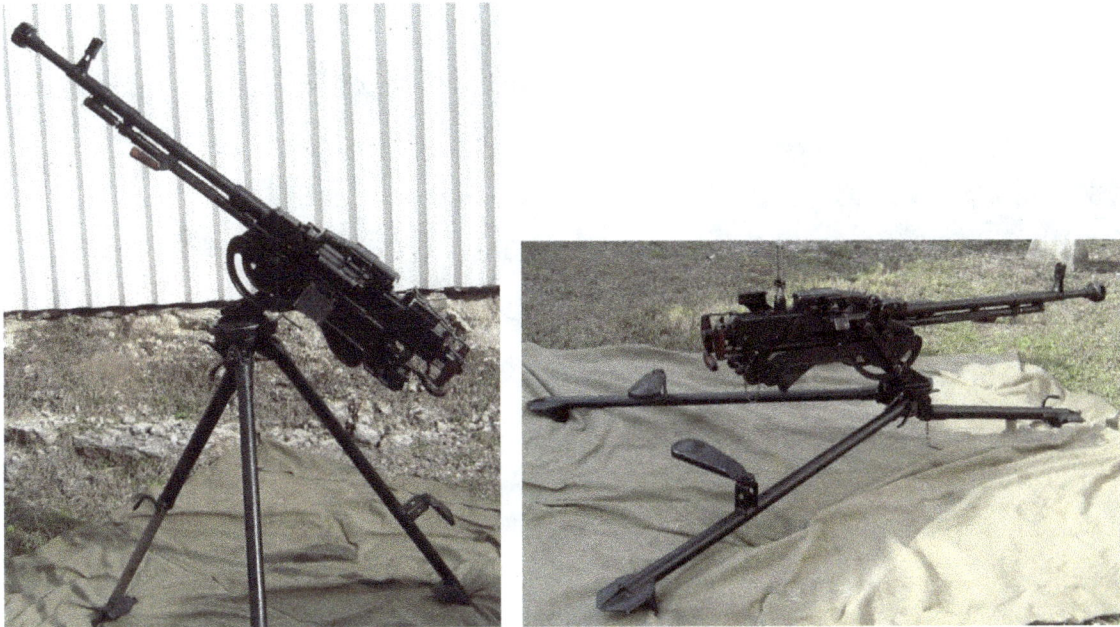

Figure 3-11 Tripod positions

The legs can be adjusted to suit the firing position (Figure 3-11).

Figure 3-12a & 3-12b Windage adjustments

Windage adjustments: For minor adjustments left and right, you can use the deflection wheel on the cradle; for major adjustments, loosen the locking ring on the cradle and tripod mating platform, point the weapon, and then retighten when oriented correctly (Figures 3-12a and 3-12b).

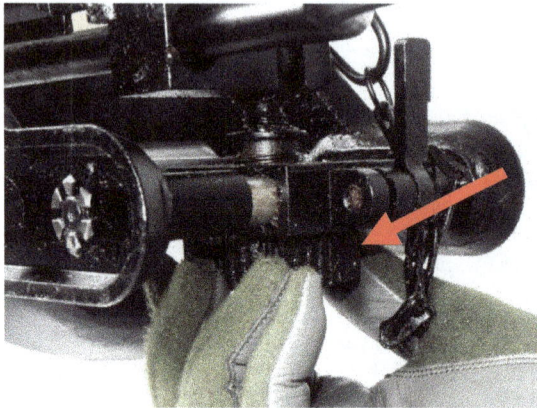

Figure 3-13a   **Figure 3-13b**

Elevation adjustments

Elevation adjustments: For minor adjustments up and down, you can use the elevation wheel on the cradle; for major adjustments, loosen the locking lever on the cradle, point the weapon, and then retighten when oriented correctly (Figures 3-13a and 3-13b).

Loading the DShKM MG

Figure 3-14 Cleared DShKM

A. Clear the weapon as described previously and leave the feed-tray cover open, bolt forward, and weapon on fire (Figure 3-14).

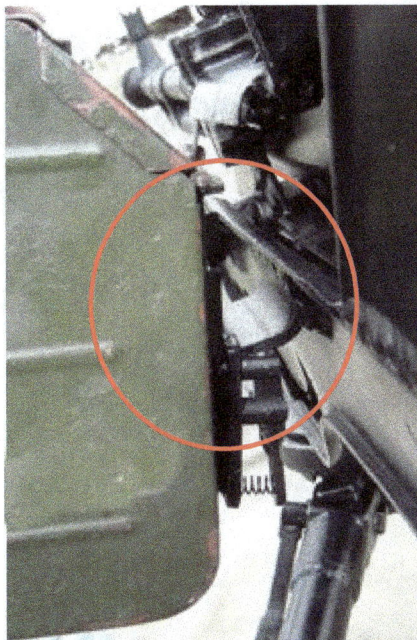

Figure 3-15 Locked on ammunition can

B. Lock on a can of ammunition by setting the top lip on the left side receiver lip and rotate the can down to lock into place (Figure 3-15).

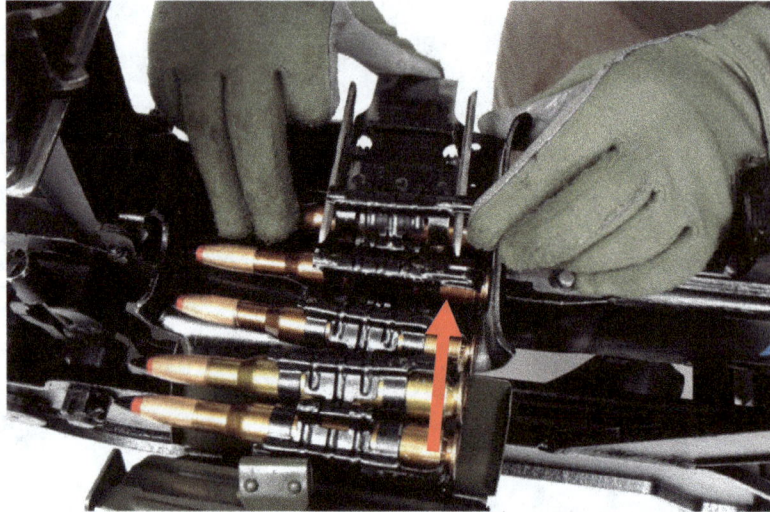

Figure 3-16 Loading the DShKM

C. With the weapon pointed in a safe direction, place the link as shown (feeds from left to right and brass case down onto the feed tray and link up) with the first round up against the feed tray guide limiter and insert the link separators under the link against the cartridge. This will separate the cartridge from the link when the action is cycled/fired (Figure 3-16).

Figure 3-17 Ammunition belt in loaded position

D. Hold the belt in place and shut the feed tray cover (Figure 3-17).

Figure 3-18 Feed operating lever on slide stud

E. When you shut the feed tray pay attention to the yoke of the feed operating lever and ensure it in on the slide stud when fully closed (Figure 3-18). NOTE- this allows it to feed the belt to the receiver during firing.

NOTE-- Loading the DShKM without opening the cover can be done by placing the starter tab on the ammunition belt into the left side of the feed tray and pulling it to the right till the first round is held by the belt holding pawl. If the bolt happens to be forward you must pull it back by the operating rod once the ammo is loaded.

Firing the DShKM MG

A. Prepare the weapon for firing by lubricating it. Motor oil (30-40 weight), made for high pressures and high temperatures is what is needed and is viscous enough to stick. Synthetic oil if you can find it, is even better. Pour it on the feed tray to ensure it is dragged into the chamber and working parts as you fire.

B. Orient downrange or towards the threat; set your sight to the estimated range to target.

Figure 3-19 FIRE position for DShKM safety lever

C. Push down and rotate the safety lever to the rear (fire position) (Figure 3-19).

D. Orient your sights onto the target, estimate the range and adjust the rear sight to that estimate. Maintain proper sight alignment and sight placement onto the target.

E. Firmly slap the trigger to the rear and hold the trigger straight back and attempt to not interrupt the sight picture. When you release, do it all at one time not slowly. As the weapon has severe recoil, ensure the tripod and or mounting system is as tight as possible to allow for a reasonable beaten zone of impact, i.e. sandbagged or spiked down. Do not "press or milk the trigger" as this action will cause malfunctions and damage the sear.

F. Maintain a 6- to 10-round burst and understand you might need to have an assistant gunner to tighten and/or adjust your mount to stay on target between bursts.

Figure 3-19 DShKM Muzzle flash

Figure 3-20 SAFE position for DShKM safety lever

G. When you have completed firing the machine gun, place the safety lever into the safe position (forward). Typically, if you have been firing at the enemy, not a target on a range, you should move. Everyone within miles will see and hear you shoot the DShKM (Figure 3-21).

Unloading the DShKM MG

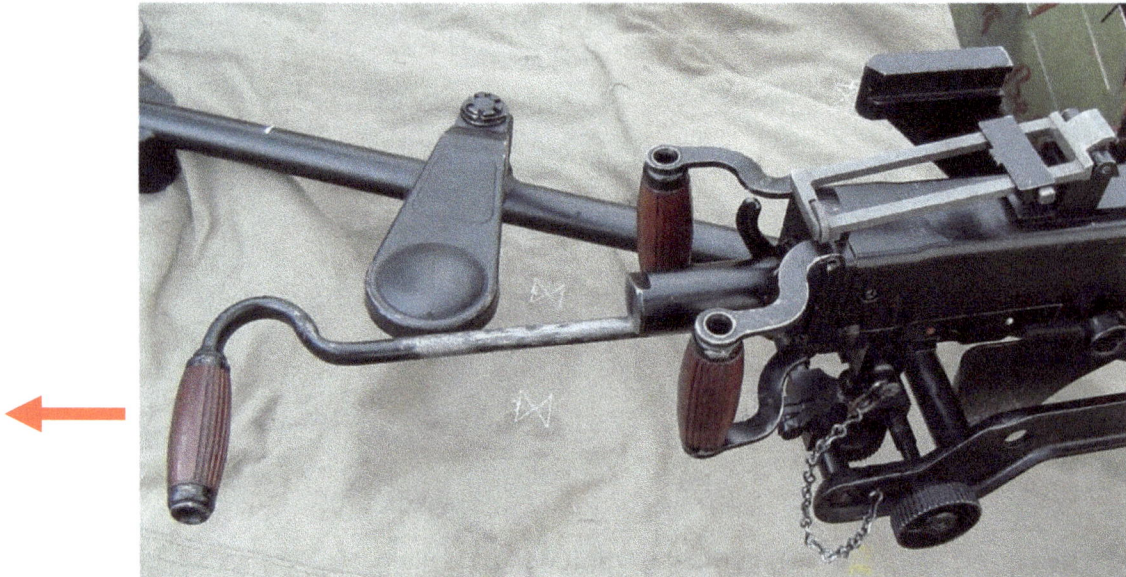

Figure 3-22 Operating rod

A. Pull the bolt to the rear by the charging handle (Figure 3-22).

Figure 3-23 Safety lever

B. Place the weapon is on safe, safety lever forward (Figure 3-23).

Figure 3-24a Feed tray catch

Figure 3-24b   **Figure 3-24c**
Feed tray locked in the fully up position

C. To open the feed tray cover by pushing the cover catch and lock it in the up position (Figures 3-24a - 3-24c).

Figure 3-25a Location of belt prior to unloading

| **Figure 3-25b** | **Figure 3-25c** |

Remove ammunition and belt from feed tray

D. Lift up the feed tray cover; remove any belt in the mechanism (Figures 4-25a - 4-25c).

Figure 3-26 Opening the feed tray

E. Lift up the feed tray; remove any round in the mechanism if one is present (shouldn't be unless you have a failure to extract) (Figure 3-26).

Figure 3-27 Inspecting the chamber

F. Inspect the face of the bolt and chamber to ensure it is clear of ammunition (Figure 3-27).

G. Rotate the safety to fire.

H. While holding the operating handle, press the trigger and ease the bolt forward, then place back on safe.

NOTE: you may use the method below if the charging handle is not operating.

Figure 3-28 Expedient charging handle

1. Use a spent casing to actuate the bolt by inserting the rear of the casing into the exposed bolt receptacle (Figure 3-28).

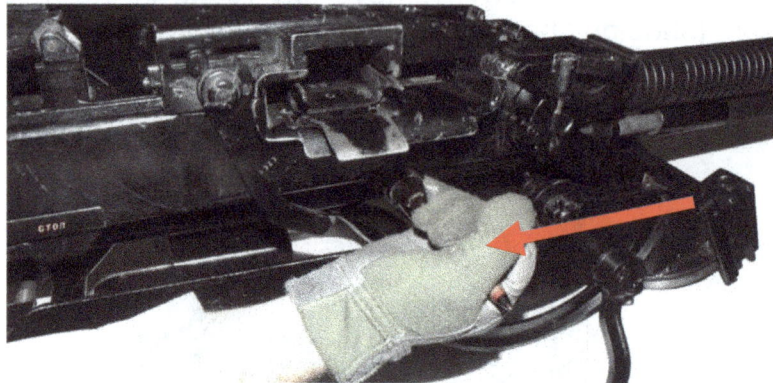

Figure 3-29 Expedient charging handle usage

2. Pull the bolt to the rear or ride it forward on the empty chamber (Figure 3-29).

I. Close the cover and lower the rear sight.

Section 4

Performance Problems

Malfunction and Immediate Action Procedures

Malfunctions are usually preventable through good practices, but they may still occur out of the blue from time to time. Of course, you hope it is on the practice range, but you should treat each one as if you are in a life-or-death situation. Practicing proper and effective corrective actions will allow you to be more confident in your weapon handling. In stressful situations, you can become much more stressed due to an unforeseen malfunction that can be dealt with easily.

Proper training will do more to save your life than technology. Malfunction drills must fix the problem 100% of the time (excluding a weapon stoppage—broken weapon) the first time performed. You must look at the weapon and identify the problem (obviously the weapon is not functioning as you need it to, so you must transition to another weapon or rectify the situation). It is a non-functioning weapon at this point—fix it.

FAILURE TO FIRE: This malfunction occurs when the belt has loaded a dud cartridge, belt was not advanced far enough during loading or you don't have a bolt in the weapon (don't laugh, saw it!).

SYMPTOM - You pull the trigger to the rear and you hear the bolt slam into the chamber with no round firing. This can also happen in the firing of a burst, but the symptom is the same.

Figure 4-1 Rack the charging handle to the rear and push back forward

A. **RACK -** The universal fix for this is to recharge the weapon (by pulling the operating handle to the rear and returning it forward) with the charging handle and watch for an unfired round to be ejected (Figure 4-1); maintain muzzle to threat orientation.

B. **BANG -** Attempt to refire. If it does not refire, move to the failure-to-feed malfunction corrective actions.

FAILURE TO FEED: If weapon does not refire after a failure to fire that was recharged, then you must pull the bolt to the rear, place the weapon on safe, open the feed-tray cover, and re-lay your ammunition belt. As you are doing this step, look for any cartridges or casings in the action and/or chamber. Once you have re-laid your ammunition belt, close the cover. If you are to attempt to fire again, place the weapon on fire, sight at the target, and attempt to engage.

NOTE: If the primer of the cartridge has been struck, then the ammunition is probably at fault; if the primer of the cartridge has not been struck, then the weapon is probably at fault.

FAILURE TO EXTRACT: This malfunction is very common with the DShKM and is the most time consuming to correct. This malfunction is created when the spent casing is not extracted from the chamber (due to faulty sized/manufactured ammo, dirty ammo or a pitted chamber) and the next round to be loaded is rammed from the magazine into the rear of the stuck casing. Below is the breakdown of the corrective action to restore your weapon back to operation.

STEP ONE - With your finger off the trigger, pull the charging handle back to lock the bolt to the rear, and place the weapon on safe.

STEP TWO - Open the feed-tray cover; remove any ammunition belts and loose ammunition from the feed tray.

STEP THREE - Lift the feed tray and inspect the chamber and receiver for casings. The casing that was not extracted will be seen still seated in the chamber.

STEP FOUR - Either you or your assistant gunner needs to assemble the steel cleaning rod. Once assembled slide the rod down the bore from the muzzle end until it contacts the stuck casing. With a hammer tap the rod until the casing is driven out of the chamber. Once the casing is out of the chamber, remove the steel rod from the muzzle and perform a normal loading procedure and attempt to refire. If time permits, clean the chamber and ensure your ammunition belts are clean and free of dirt.

RECOIL SPRING FAILURE: If there are still problems, the recoil spring in the trigger group probably needs to be changed as it has a really bad tendency to shatter. Once that part breaks the gun will still work but you will start to encounter all of the above problems. Then a broken piston is only a matter of time. Replace the next time you disassemble and inspect for breakages.

Finally, it comes down to maintenance. Most of the ammo that is shot is poor quality; you are not supposed to fire captured ammo, but the reality of it is that it gets in the supply train from time to time. The captured ammo has corrosive primers and will pock mark the chamber, causing the failure-to-extract malfunction which is the most common complaint with the DShKM. DO NOT FIRE ANY CAPTURED AMMUNITION! Inspect your chamber on all barrels as the more pitted they are the more casing will stick on extraction. And yes you should headspace the barrels to the weapons by checking with the gauge and seeing which barrels go with which receivers. VSS is the only place I have seen a 12.7x108mm headspace gauge set.

Appendix A - Ammunition

<u>12.7 x 108mm</u> *Degtyarev* heavy machine gun ammunition. Inspect all cartridges for uniformity, cleanliness, and serviceability. Check all for undented primers, and only use issued ammunition.

The Russian/Soviet <u>12.7 x 108mm</u> cartridge was introduced in 1934 as a competitor to the German 13mm antitank round and the U.S. .50 Browning MG (12.7 x 99mm). The round was used in the WWII DK and DShK-38 machinegun in 50 round belts for anti aircraft use and against light armored ground targets. Rate of fire of the gas operated weapon was 600 rpm, out of a 4 right turn threaded 1070mm/ 42" barrel, muzzle velocity was 860 - 880m/s (2821–2887 fps) and the operation temperature could vary from -50°C to +50°C (-58 F to 122 F).

It was also used in the Universalny Berezina aircraft machinegun in WWII that could be fixed to aircrafts like the I-16 and I-153 in synchronized (UBS), wing mounted (UBK) and turret mounted (UBT) installations. The gun had a rate of fire of 1050 rpm, but in the synchronized version that rate dropped to 800 rpm. The gas operated UB was the best gun of its class, lighter (21kg/46.3 lbs.) and faster firing than any other guns with similar ammunition performance.

The post WWII guns YakB-12.7 and YakBYu-12.7, original designation 9A624, are 4 barrel guns and are mounted on helicopters like the Mi-24. The first gun weights 45kg / 99 lbs. and fires 4000-4500rds/min, the later 60kg/132 lbs. and fires 4000-5000rds/min. Both guns are rotary machineguns operated by gas pressure. The Afanassijef-12.7 (A-12.7) machinegun also uses this ammo. This single barrel gas operated gun weights 28kg/62 lbs. Ammunition belts for the A-12.7 have a linkage of 1x B-32, 3x BZT and 1x MDZ.

The Russian long range sniper rifles V-94, OSV-96 and SVN-98 also use this type of ammunition with a special solid brass bullet similar to the U.S. M33 type. The V-94 sniper rifle has been introduced in the Russian army and used by Special Forces. The other two rifles are new developments.

The NSVT machinegun, mounted on many armored vehicles (e.g. T-64 and T-70), still uses this caliber. The barrel has 8 right-hand grooves resulting in an improved fire-rate of 750rpm. The 50 round ammo-belts used a linkage of 3 B-32 to 1 BZT-44 (3 API to 1 API-T). These bullets have the following armor-piercing effect: 90% of all bullets penetrate a 20mm / .8" thick armor plate at 100m. The capability of the tungsten carbide core bullet BS is said to be about 7 times higher than standard bullets. 75% of all bullets ignite the petrol placed behind the 20mm armor plate.

A HEI (high explosive/incendiary) bullet, the MDZ is used for AA purpose. It has a flat nose and mainly uses an air-compression type of fuse. It is filled with HE or HE + incendiary charge and a small blasting cap. Actually 5 types of MDZ projectiles are known: The first has a screwed-on air compression fuse, the second a fuse with striker pin and setback safety device. The third has the air compression tube within the projectile jacket and is closed with a brass washer at the flat tip. The fourth is basically the same as the second, but has a streamlined outline and is produced post WWII only. The fifth has also a tracer and is filled with an incendiary charge in the nose and a blasting cap and HE below.

The construction of the "ZP" instantaneous incendiary projectile is also not known, so the fifth MDZ type could actually be the ZP type.

Cartridges are packed in 80 rounds per sealed metal box with two of these boxes per wooden container. Blank cartridges are packed in 95/190 pieces. For Navy use, 170 cartridges are separated into two metal boxes with those packed in a wooden box. These boxes have the caliber, type of bullet, Lot.-No., number of rounds and type of propellant painted on them. The later measures 480 x 350 x 160mm (18.8" x 13.8" x 6.3") and weights 29kg/64 lbs.

Ammunition is exported from Russia to over forty countries and also is manufactured in Bulgaria, China, former Czechoslovakia, Egypt, Iran, Pakistan, Romania and Yugoslavia.

Ammunition Commonly Used-
12.7mm CARTRIDGE WITH BS ARMOR-PIERCING INCENDIARY BULLET (DESIGNATION 7BZ-1)

This cartridge is designed to engage lightly armored ground targets, weapon emplacements and targets located behind light barriers at ranges of up to 1,000 m, concentrated infantry and motor transport at ranges of up to 1,500 m, and low-flying air targets at altitudes of up to 1,500 m. It ignites the B-70 gasoline. It is fired from NSV, NSVT and DShKM machine guns. The bullet is painted red with a black tip.

Caliber,	12.7 x 108mm
Weight, grams:	
cartridge-	141 gm
bullet-	55.4 gm
Cartridge length-	147 mm
Muzzle velocity-	818 m/s

12.7mm CARTRIDGE WITH MDZ INSTANTANEOUS ACTION INCENDIARY BULLET (DESIGNATION 7-Z-2)

This cartridge is designed to fight low flying air targets and to set them on fire. It ignites the B-70 gasoline. It is fired from NSV, NSVT and DShKM large caliber machine guns. The bullet is painted red.

Caliber-	12.7 x 108mm
Weight, grams:	

cartridge-	127 gm
bullet-	43 gm
Cartridge length-	147 mm
Muzzle velocity-	828 m/s
Case brass	

12.7mm CARTRIDGE WITH BZT-44 ARMOR-PIERCING INCENDIARY TRACER BULLET (DESIGNATION 57-BZT-542) AND WITH BZT-44M MODERNIZED ARMORPIERCING INCENDIARY TRACER BULLET (DESIGNATION 57-BZT-542M*)

This cartridge is designed to designate targets, adjust fire and ignite targets containing combustible materials. It ignites the B-70 gasoline. It is fired from NSV, NSVT, DShKM and A-12.7 large caliber machine guns. The bullet point is painted violet and red.

Caliber-	12.7 x 108 mm
Weight, grams:	
cartridge-	128 gm
bullet-	44 gm
Cartridge length-	147 mm
Muzzle velocity-	818 m/s
Minimum tracer burning time- 3 seconds	
Trace initiation from muzzle face- 50 meters	
Case brass	

12.7mm CARTRIDGE WITH B-32 ARMOR-PIERCING INCENDIARY BULLET (DESIGNATION 57-BZ-542)

This cartridge is designed to engage lightly armored ground targets (armored personnel carriers), weapon emplacements and targets behind light barriers at ranges of up to 1,000 m, concentrated infantry and motor transport at ranges of up to 1,500 m and low flying air targets at altitudes of up to 1,500 m. It ignites the B-70 gasoline. It is fired from NSV, NSVT and DShKM machine guns, as well as the OSV-96 sniper rifle. The bullet point is painted black and red.

Caliber-	12.7 x 108 mm
Weight, grams:	
cartridge-	133.5 gm
bullet-	48.2 gm
Cartridge length-	147 mm
Muzzle velocity-	818 m/s
Case brass	

12.7mm 1SL DUPLEX CARTRIDGE (DESIGNATION 9-A-4012)

This cartridge is designed to engage manpower and unarmored ground materiel at ranges of 1,000 to 1,500 m. It is fired from the YakB-12.7 aircraft machine gun

installed on Mi-24D and Mi-24V helicopters. The bullet is not painted.
Caliber-   12.7 x 108 mm
Weight, grams:
cartridge-   145 gm
bullet-   31 gm
Cartridge length-   147 mm
Muzzle velocity of first/second bullet- 735/680 m/s
Case brass

12.7mm 1SLT DUPLEX TRACER CARTRIDGE (DESIGNATION 9-A-4427)

This cartridge is designed to designate targets, adjust fire and engage manpower and unarmored materiel at ranges of at least 1,000 m. It is fired from the YakB-12.7 aircraft machine gun installed on Mi-24D and Mi-24V helicopters. The bullet point is painted green.
Caliber-   12.7 x 108 mm
Weight, grams:
cartridge-   142 gm
first/second bullet   31/27gm
Cartridge length-   147 mm
Muzzle velocity of first/second bullet- 730/700 m/s
Range of tracer burning time- 1,000 meters
Min range of trace- 2.9 seconds
Case brass

Appendix B - Ammunition Comparison

9x18mm
Makarov

9x19mm
Luger

7.62x25mm
Tokarev

.45 ACP

PISTOLS AND SUBMACHINE GUNS

**Size Comparison of
NATO vs. Non-Standard
Ammunition**

5.56x
45mm

5.45x
39mm

5.56x
45mm

7.62x
39mm

7.62x
51mm

7.62x
54R mm

12.7x
99mm

12.7x
108mm

ASSAULT RIFLES

SNIPER RIFLES & MACHINE GUNS

Appendix C - Non-Standard Ammunition Packaging & Markings

Packaging

Russian small arms cartridges are packed in sealed sheet-metal containers, with two containers per wooden crate. Older Russian production used rectangular containers of heavy gauge galvanized iron with soldered seams. Around 1959, the introduction of painted, rolled edge, rounded corner, tin plate 'sardine can' containers became the standard.

Metal and wooden crates have standardized markings that identify the contents as to caliber, functional type, cartridge case material, quantity and cartridge/powder lot data. Specialized cartridges are further identified by a color code consisting of one or two color stripes which correspond to bullet tip color. AP cartridges with tungsten carbide cores are identified by two concentric circles instead of color stripes. Russian cartridge designation, packaging and marking practices are generally followed by former Soviet-Bloc countries; each, however, has introduced some modifications in designation and marking. Russian ammunition packaging can be distinguished from Bulgarian packaging, which also carries Cyrillic markings, primarily by the different factory codes. The factory code on the container also appears in the headstamp of the cartridges in the container.

Steel Ammo Tins
(Sardine Cans)

Wood Ammo Crate (Case)
(Contains 2 Tins + Opener)

Cartridge quantities and weights of wooden crates

Country	Manufacturer	Caliber	Rounds /Crate	Crate Weight
Czech Rep.	Sellier and Bellot	14.5 x 114	210	53 kg.
India	OFB	14.5 x 114	60	15.5 kg.
Russia	Unknown	14.5 x 114	80	23 kg.
Bulgaria	Arsenal	12.7 x 108	200	29 kg.
Bulgaria	Arsenal	12.7 x 108	200	32 kg.
Pakistan	POF	12.7 x 108	280	42 kg.
Russia	Unknown	12.7 x 108	190	29 kg.
Russia	Novosibirsk	12.7 x 108	160	25 kg.
Bulgaria	Arsenal	7.62 x 54(R)	880	25 kg.
Czech Rep.	Sellier and Bellot	7.62 x 54(R)	800	24 kg.
Russia	Novosibirsk	7.62 x 54(R)	880	26 kg.
Russia	Novosibirsk	7.62 x 54(R)	600	21 kg.
Russia	Unknown	7.62 x 54(R)	880	26 kg.
Serbia	Prvi Partizan	7.62 x 54(R)	1,200	39 kg.
Czech Rep.	Sellier and Bellot	7.62 x 39	1,200	28 kg.
Pakistan	POF	7.62 x 39	1,750	39 kg.
Russia	Barnaul	7.62 x 39	1,320	30 kg.
Serbia	Prvi Partizan	7.62 x 39	1,260	29 kg.
Sudan	STC	7.62 x 39	1,500	28.1 kg.
Ukraine	Lugansk	7.62 x 39	1,320	30 kg.
Yugoslavia	Igman Zavod	7.62 x 39	1,260	28 kg.
Yugoslavia	Igman Zavod	7.62 x 39	1,120	27.5 kg.
Russia	Unknown	5.45 x 39	2,160	29 kg.
Ukraine	Lugansk	5.45 x 39	2,160	29 kg.

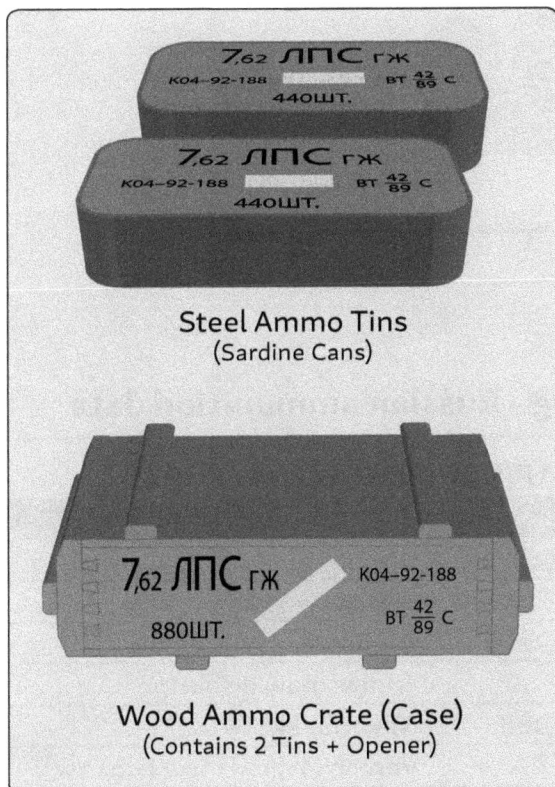

Non-Standard Ammunition tin and crate marking - diagrams

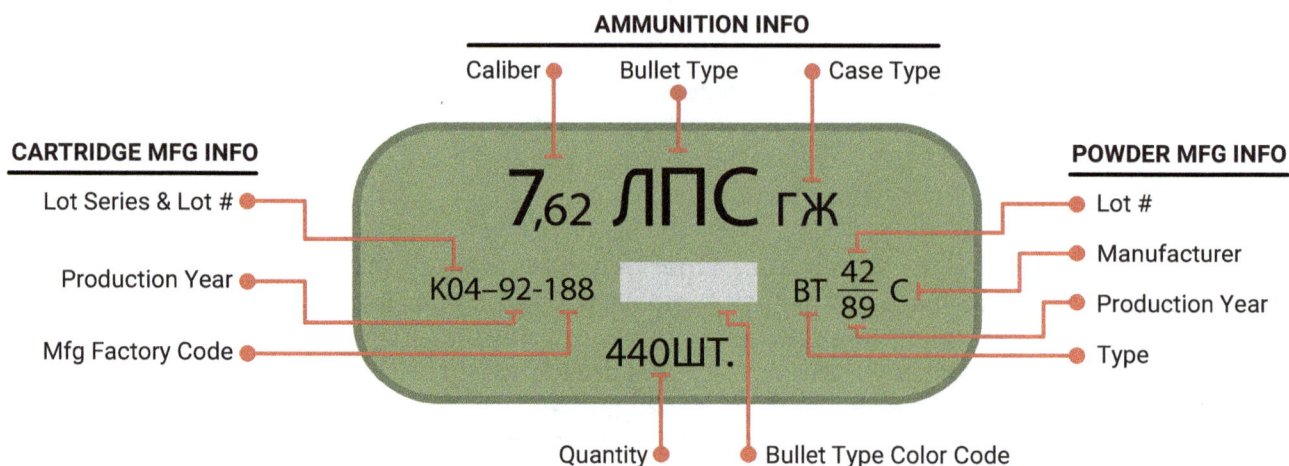

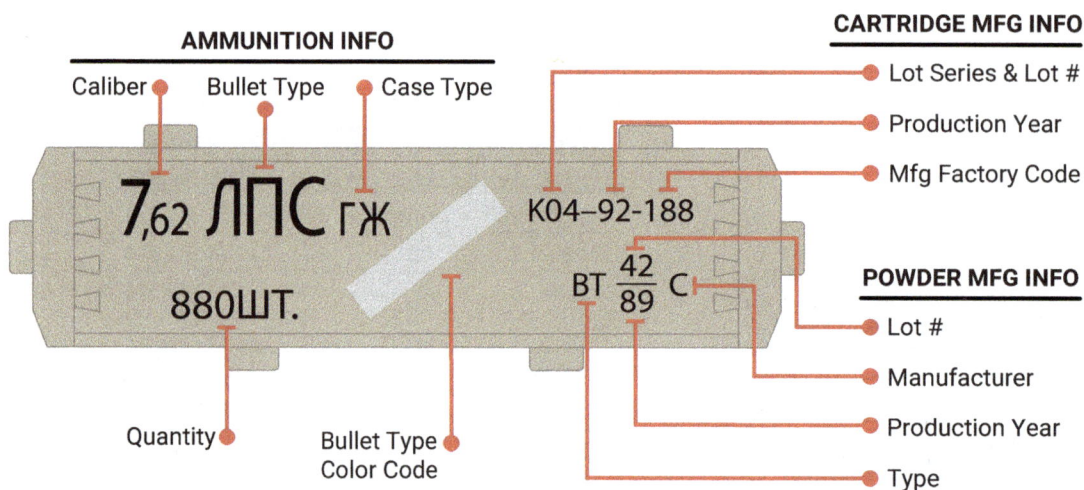

AMMUNITION INFO

Caliber · Bullet Type · Case Type

CARTRIDGE MFG INFO

Lot Series & Lot #

Production Year

Mfg Factory Code

POWDER MFG INFO

Lot #

Manufacturer

Production Year

Type

7,62 ЛПС ГЖ

K04–92–188

BT $\frac{42}{89}$ C

440ШТ.

Quantity · Bullet Type Color Code

AMMUNITION INFO

Caliber · Bullet Type · Case Type

CARTRIDGE MFG INFO

Lot Series & Lot #

Production Year

Mfg Factory Code

7,62 ЛПС ГЖ

880ШТ.

K04–92–188

BT $\frac{42}{89}$ C

POWDER MFG INFO

Lot #

Manufacturer

Production Year

Type

Quantity · Bullet Type Color Code

Non-Standard Ammunition tin and crate marking - Russian ammunition data

CASE TYPE MARKINGS

Mark	Meaning
ГЖ	Bimetallic case (gilding metal clad steel)
ГЛ	Brass case
ГС	Steel case

CARTRIDGE MFG FACTORY CODES

Code	Location
3	Ulyanovsk
17	Barnaul
38	Yuryuzan
60	Frunze (now Bishkek)
188	Novosibirsk
270	Voroshilovgrad (now Luhansk)
304	Lugansk
539	Tula
711	Klimovsk
T	Tula

Non-Standard Ammunition tin and crate marking - Russian ammunition data

BULLET TYPE MARKINGS

Mark	Meaning
Б Б-30 Б-32 БП	Armor-piercing
Б3	Armor-piercing incendiary
Б3Т Б3Т-44	Armor-piercing incendiary tracer
БС БС-40 БС-41	Armor-piercing with special core of tungsten carbide instead of carbon steel
БСТ	Armor-piercing with tungsten carbide core with added tracer
БТ	Armor-piercing tracer
Д	Heavy (long-range) with lead core instead of carbon steel
З ЗП	Incendiary
Л	Lightweight bullet
ЛПС	Light ball bullet with mild steel core
МДЗ	High explosive incendiary
П П-41	Spotting / ranging
ПЗ	Incendiary spotting / ranging
ПП	Enhanced penetration
ПС	Spotting / ranging with mild steel core
ПТ	Spotting / ranging tracer
СНБ	Armor-piercing sniper
Т Т-30 Т-45 Т-46	Tracer
57-У-322 57-У-323	Cartridge with higher powder charge
57-У-423	High-pressure cartridge
57-Х-322 57-Х-323 57-Х-340	Blank cartridge
57-НЕ-УЧ	Training cartridge
7Н1	Sniper bullet

BULLET TYPE COLOR CODES (Ammunition up to 14.5mm)

Color	Meaning
No color	Ball
White tip	Reference Ball
Silver tip	Light ball with steel core
Yellow tip	Heavy ball, or ball with torpedo base (on 7.62x54R)
Blue tip + white band	Short range ball 14.5x114 (only Hungarian and Czech)
Green tip + white band	Short range, tracer, (only Czech designation, only found on 7.62x39 with round nose)
Green tip	Tracer
Green tip & head-stamp or entire cartridge green	Subsonic ammunition for silencer-weapons
Red tip	Spotting charge, incendiary
Red tip + white band	Short range tracer ball 14.5x114 (only Hungarian designation)
Entire bullet red	High explosive bullet (7.62x54R after 1945)
Entire bullet red	High explosive bullet (on 12.7 and 14.5mm)
Magenta tip + red band	Armor piercing incendiary tracer
Black tip + red band	Armor piercing incendiary
Black tip + red shell	Armor piercing incendiary with tungsten carbide core
Black tip + yellow band	Armor piercing incendiary Phosphorus 12.7
Black tip	Armor piercing

** The bullet tip color codes in the table above will be the same color codes on the tins or crates, but they will be color stripes on the packaging.

Example:

CARTRIDGE
Black Tip + Red Band

TIN or CRATE
Black Stripe + Red Stripe

Appendix D - Non-Standard Weapon Identification Markings

General Identification Markings

There are various identification markings found on non-standard weapons. Typically the markings will provide some or all of the following information:
- factory name or stamp (proof mark)
- caliber & serial number
- selector lever markings/symbols
- rear sight mark/symbol

NOTE: Data tables are not all inclusive, but they cover the more common weapon manufacturers.

Selector Lever Markings on Kalashnikov Rifles

Upper/ Safe Symbol	Mid/ Full-Auto Symbol	Lower/ Semi-Auto Symbol	Country
	Д	1	Albania
	L	D	Albania
	AB	ЕД	Bulgaria
	L	D	China
	进	单	China
	30	1	Czechoslovakia
	آلی	خودی	Egypt
	D	E	Egypt
	D	E	East Germany
	∞	1	Hungary
أ	ص	م	Iraq
	련	단	North Korea
	C	P	Poland
	Z	O	Poland
S	A	R	Romania
S	FA	FF	Romania
	1	3	Romania
	ЛР	ОГОНЬ	Russia
	АВ	ОД	Russia
U	R	Ј	Yugo/Serbia

Rear Sight Marks on Kalashnikov Rifles

Symbol	Country
D	Albania
П	Bulgaria
D	China
N	East Germany
A	Hungary
口	North Korea
S	Poland
P	Romania
П	Russia
O	Yugo/Serbia

DShK Selector Markings

Figure A-1 Unknown
RED = FIRE   WHITE = SAFE

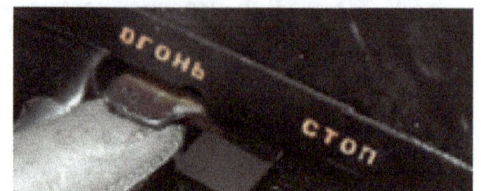

Figure A-2 Russian
Огонь translates to FIRE
Стоп translates to STOP

Non-Standard Weapon Identification Markings

Factory Stamps and Countries of Manufacture

The table of symbols below are factory stamps (proof marks) for non-standard weapons. The symbols will identify the country of manufacture of the weapon. NOTE: *This is not an all inclusive list, but it covers the more common weapon manufacturers.*

(10) Bulgaria	(21) Bulgaria	(25) Bulgaria	China
(386) China	36 China	66 China	China
Egypt	East Germany	(3) East Germany	(K3) East Germany
East Germany	(06) East Germany	Iraq	Iraq
North Korea	North Korea	(11) Poland	Romania
Russia	Russia	Russia	Russia
Russia	Russia	Russia	Russia
Yugoslavia/Serbia	M.70.AB2 Yugoslavia/Serbia	ZASTAVA-KRAGUJEVAC Yugoslavia/Serbia	

Appendix E - Non-standard weapons theory overview

There are three key concepts to understand when manipulating non-standard weapons. These simple and logical concepts are:

1. CYCLE OF OPERATIONS
2. OPERATING SYSTEMS
3. LOCKING SYSTEMS

> Firearm design trends are shared across region, manufacturer and class of weapon and are relatively obvious to recognize.
>
> Keep in mind that firearms are essentially simple machines that harness the energy created by the fired cartridge to operate the system.

CYCLE OF OPERATIONS (COO)

The cycle of operations is a crucial basis for understanding how the weapon operates and for function/malfunction diagnosis. Each specific malfunction will correspond to a specific step or sometimes two in the COO. A failure in the system at a certain point, will by default, cause a failure of omission of all subsequent steps. (example – a failure to properly extract will manifest as a failure to eject.)

The COO will vary based on the type of operating and locking systems. Once the operating and locking systems of the weapon are known, the COO is logical.

The examples below all start from a standard reference point: the weapon is loaded, charged, placed on fire and the trigger is pulled.

'Cycle of Operations' Examples:

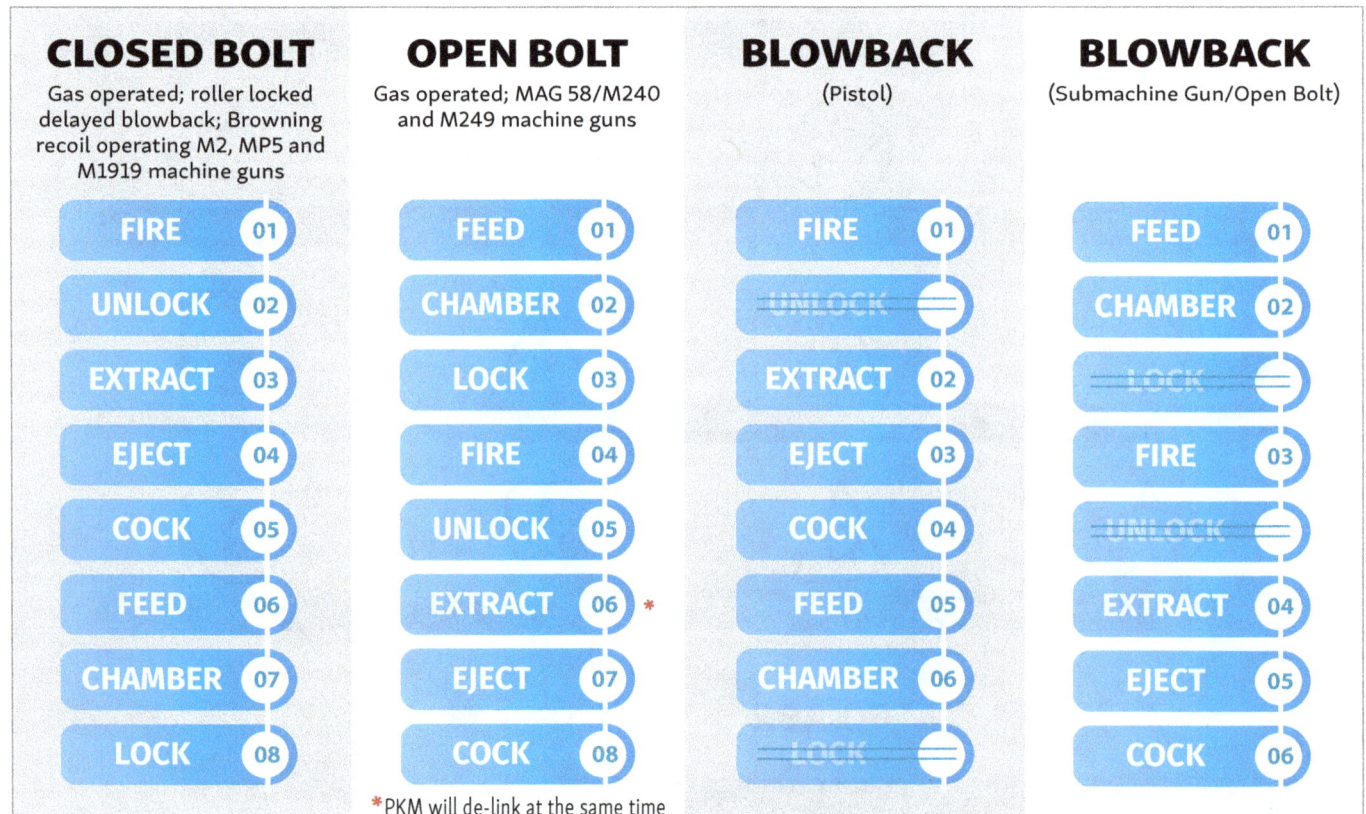

CLOSED BOLT	**OPEN BOLT**	**BLOWBACK**	**BLOWBACK**
Gas operated; roller locked delayed blowback; Browning recoil operating M2, MP5 and M1919 machine guns	Gas operated; MAG 58/M240 and M249 machine guns	(Pistol)	(Submachine Gun/Open Bolt)
FIRE 01	FEED 01	FIRE 01	FEED 01
UNLOCK 02	CHAMBER 02	~~UNLOCK~~	CHAMBER 02
EXTRACT 03	LOCK 03	EXTRACT 02	~~LOCK~~
EJECT 04	FIRE 04	EJECT 03	FIRE 03
COCK 05	UNLOCK 05	COCK 04	~~UNLOCK~~
FEED 06	EXTRACT 06 *	FEED 05	EXTRACT 04
CHAMBER 07	EJECT 07	CHAMBER 06	EJECT 05
LOCK 08	COCK 08	~~LOCK~~	COCK 06

*PKM will de-link at the same time

Non-standard weapons theory overview *(continued ...)*

⚙ OPERATING SYSTEMS

1. **Direct Impingement**- a type of gas operation that directs gas from a fired cartridge directly to the bolt carrier or slide assembly to cycle the action. (AR-15/M4 variants)

2. **Long-stroke piston system**- the piston is mechanically fixed to the bolt group and moves through the entire operating cycle. (AK variants)

3. **Short-stroke piston system (tappet system)**- the piston moves separately from the bolt group. It may directly push the bolt group parts as n the M1 carbine or operate through a connecting rod. (HK 416, AR180, POF, LWRC, FN FAL)

4. **Blowback**- the system of operation for self-loading firearms that obtains energy from the motion of the cartridge case as it is pushed to the rear by expanding gases created by the ignition of the propellant charge. (STEN, Makarov, M3 Grease Gun)

5. **Short recoil action**- the barrel and slide recoil only a short distance before they unlock and separate. The barrel stops quickly, and the slide continues rearward compressing the recoil spring and performing extraction, ejection and finally feeding a fresh round from the magazine in the counter recoil phase. During the last portion of its forward travel, the slide locks into the barrel and pushes the barrel back into battery. *(This is found in most handguns chambered for 9x19mm Parabellum or greater caliber. Smaller calibers, 9x18mm Makarov and below, generally use the blowback method of operation due to lower chamber pressure and associated simplicity of design.)

6. **Roller-locked, delayed-blowback**- when the bolt is closed, the rollers carried in the bolt are wedged into the receiver recesses. On firing, the rollers must be forced out of the recesses at great mechanical disadvantage, delaying the opening of the bolt, even with full power 7.62mm NATO (.308 Winchester) rifle cartridges used in the G3/HK 91 (G3, HK 91, HK 93, HK 53, MP5 variants)

7. **Inertia operated systems**- the bolt body is separated from the locked bolt body to remain stationary while the recoiling gun and locked bolt head moves rearward. This movement compresses the spring between the bolt head and bolt body, storing the energy required to cycle the action. Benelli shotguns.

Non-standard weapons theory overview *(continued ...)*

🔒 LOCKING SYSTEMS

1. **None** - all blowback pistols and some submachine guns – (STEN, UZI, M3 Grease Gun, Makarov, and CZ 82)

2. **Roller** - (HK variants, MG3, MG34, MG 42 and CZ 52)

3. **Rotating bolt** - (AK, Stoner, M60, and M249)

4. **Tilting bolt** - (SKS, FN FAL and MAG 58/M240)

5. **Tilting barrel** - (Tokarev TT33, Sig variants, M1911 variants and Glock variants)

6. **Rotating barrel** - (MAB P15, Colt All American 2000, and Beretta 8000)

7. **Locking flaps** - (RPD, DP/DPM and DShK)

8. **Falling locking block** - (P38, M9, and VZ58)

Function check
Checking the mechanical function of a weapon by replicating, without ammunition, the firing modes from the lowest rate of fire (SAFE if applicable) to the highest in a progressive sequence (not by selector location). The parts checked are the safety/safeties, sear and disconnector.

M4A1
1. Ensure the rifle is clear
2. Charge and place the weapon on SAFE
3. Attempt to fire (weapons should not FIRE, safety is functioning)
4. Place the weapon on SEMI, pull the trigger and hold it to the rear (hammer should fall, trigger/sear functioning)
5. Maintain the trigger to the rear and cycle the bolt
6. Release the trigger and listen for a metallic click (disconnector functioning)
7. Pull the trigger again and the hammer should fall
8. Charge the weapon and place on AUTO
9. Pull the trigger and hold it to the rear then cycle the bolt more than once
10. Release the trigger and pull it again, nothing should happen (auto sear is functioning)
11. Charge the weapon then pull the trigger again and the hammer should fall
12. Function check complete

Significant visual indicators
- Any checked, knurled or serrated surface
- Any movable lever or switch
- Pins with gripping surfaces
- Index marks (two lines that need to be aligned to disassembled (CZ 75)
- Recoil spring with ends of different diameters

Appendix F- Tools and Training Tips

Essential Tools for working with DShKM Machine Guns-

- Hammer, Ball Peen, 16 ounces
- Hammer, Rubber
- Hammer, Combo – brass head and plastic head
- Wrench, Crescent, large
- Wrench, Crescent, small
- Screwdriver, set
- Pins, Cotter, small and large
- Pins, Punch, set
- Nuts, Replacement
- Cleaning Rod, Steel (old .50 BMG type)
- Headspace gauge set, GO, NO GO and FIELD

Figure F-1 Standard Soviet style tool kit

Appendix G- Good to know additional information

Training Tips

- Ensure you have inspected your components for functionality and serviceability prior to taking to the range for firing.
- Inspect your:
  - Ammunition
  - Links
  - Ammunition cans
  - Tripod- ensure you have the appropriate tripod, some are for ground use and some for anti-aircraft use. The anti-aircraft one will not allow for horizontal firing as you will need to construct a frame to hold the legs at 45 degree orientation.
  - Barrels- ensure the chambers are not pitted, should be smooth and with a mirror finish

Ammunition Can- Press down on the leaf spring like retainer which hold the top of the lid onto the bottom and rotate it out of the hooks (Figure G-1a). Open the can by lifting the lid and folding down the dust cover on the front (Figure G-1b). New link will come in double wrapped waxen paper with the link being cosmolined heavily (Figure G-1c). You may need to soak in diesel or solvent tank to break up the Cosmoline on the new link. Treat your ammo cans like your rifle magazines, not all go on smoothly and lock, check them. Once you have cans that work with the gun, mark them with a gun number and a can number, i.e. 4/1 (gun 4/can 1).

Figure G-1a
Unlocking the can

Figure G-1b
Open the can

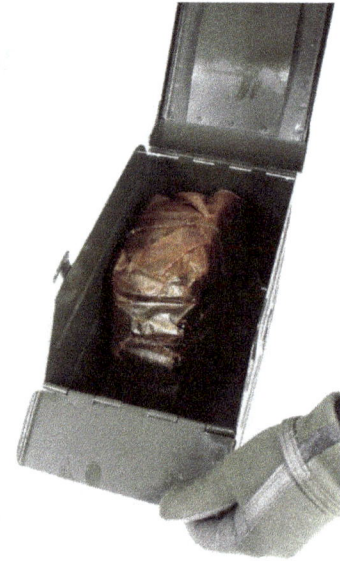

Figure G-1c
New link in the wrapper

Figure G-2a

Figure G-2b

Inspect for damaged mounting attachment points

Link Sections- Detailed in the next edition.

Link Loader- Detailed in the next edition.

Link Unloader- Detailed in the next edition.

Rear Sight Adjustment-

Figure G-3a
For gross adjustments move the slider to the desired range

Figure G-3b
For fine adjustments once on target use the elevation wheel

Figure G-3c
Keep the rear sight folded down when not in use

Field Expedient Charging Handle- you may use the method below if the charging handle is not operating.

Figure G-5a Expedient charging handle

Figure G-5b Expedient charging handle usage

Use a spent casing to actuate the bolt by inserting the rear of the casing into the exposed bolt receptacle (Figures G-5a and G-5b).

Anti-Aircraft Sight- is constructed in a way where a trained and experienced gunner can use the sight to make calculated leads on moving targets using the ringed front sight. Keep the sights folded when not in use. If the need for the AA sight to be on the gun is not warranted keep it secured in its wooden transit case.

Figure G-6 To mount or remove the AA sight onto the front/top of receiver

Figure G-7 Sight alignment for front and rear AA sight with no lead

Figure G-8 Sight alignment for front and rear AA sight with one hold lead, i.e. target flying from left to right slow or close

Figure G-9 Sight alignment for front and rear AA sight with two hold lead, i.e. target flying from left to right fast or slow and far

Shoulder Rest- Inspect the shoulder rest for serviceability by loosing and adjusting the angles and checking for tension on the cradle locking spring. Inspect the cradle attachment for nicks or deformation which would stop the rest from smoothly sliding on to the lock position.

Installing/Remove the Shoulder Rest- To install, align the rest's spring loaded female attachment with the cradle's male attachment rail and slide on until the spring locks onto the end of the rail (Figure G-10a and G-10b). To remove, lift up on the spring latch and pull the rest to the rear.

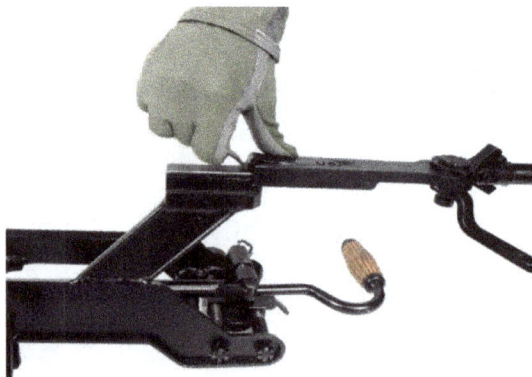

Figure G-10a
Start onto cradle rail

Figure G-10b
Push fully forward until the spring lock over the forward edge

Adjusting the vertical angle- Press the spring loaded release trigger to the rear, adjust the angle as needed, and release the trigger (Figures G-11a and G-11b).

Figure G-11a
To adjust the angle pull release to the rear

Figure G-11b
Adjust to desired angle

Adjusting the horizontal angle- Loosen the wrench lever and adjust the angle as needed and retighten (Figures G-12a and G-12b).

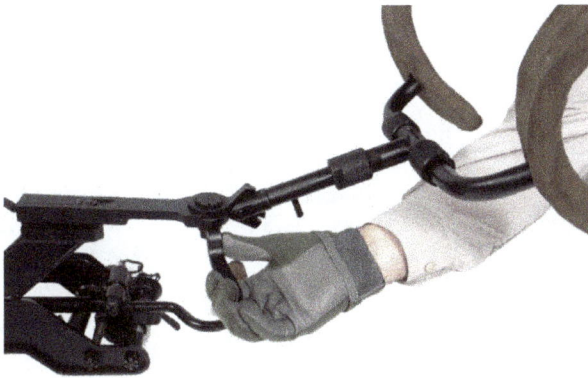

Figure G-12a
To adjust the angle loosen the lever

Figure G-12b
Adjust to desired angle and retighten